Commemorative Edition

Celebrating 100 Years of Ministry

Grand Rapids, MI

MEL TROTTER

M I N I S T R I E S

1900–2000

MAN
WITH A
MISSION

Mel Trotter and His Legacy
for the Rescue Mission Movement

Leona Hertel

kregel
PUBLICATIONS

Grand Rapids, MI 49501

Man with a Mission: Mel Trotter and His Legacy for the Rescue Mission Movement

© 2000 by Mel Trotter Ministries

Published by Kregel Publications, a division of Kregel, Inc., P.O. Box 2607, Grand Rapids, MI 49501. Kregel Publications provides trusted, biblical publications for Christian growth and service. Your comments and suggestions are valued.

For more information about Kregel Publications, visit our web site: www.kregel.com

Library of Congress Cataloging-in-Publication Data
Hertel, Leona.
   Man with a mission: Mel Trotter and his legacy for the rescue mission movement / by Leona Hertel
      p.   cm.
   1. Trotter, Melvin E. (Melvin Earnest), 1870–1940
2. Mel Trotter Ministries—Biography. I. Title.
BV2657.T7 H47   1999   266'.022'092–dc21 99-057335
                                      CIP
ISBN 0-8254-2799-1

Printed in the United States of America

1 2 3 4 5 / 04 03 02 01 00

To the thousands of volunteers
who in the past one hundred years
have given of their time and talent
and made it possible to complete
a century of service to the King.
Your name may not be included here,
but be assured that it is included
in God's record book.

Contents

Acknowledgments

THANKS TO ALL WHO supplied information that enabled me to recount highlights of the one hundred years of ministry from the Old Lighthouse. Much of the material that would today be history was discarded during the many changes of location. Rev. George Bontekoe, however, salvaged and filed a number of Mission documents, which supplemented anecdotes and memory, thereby enabling us to produce this book.

List of Testimonies and Remembrances

Introduction

REMEMBER THOSE BORING history classes in school? The hours of memorizing names, places, and dates? History is more than that. It is made up of the lives of people. And the history of any ministry is told in the way it touches and changes the lives of people.

To retell one hundred years of the history of Mel Trotter Ministries is to touch only the tip of the iceberg. Only when time ceases and we gather at the feet of Jesus will we fully comprehend what great things the Lord has done through the ministry of those who have dedicated themselves to rescuing the perishing.

What Is a Rescue Mission?

The primary purpose of a rescue mission is to save lost souls. A mission serves those who would not come into a regular church building by going out after them. An inner-city mission is often located in a depressed area; a family mission is located in a district where many families live, yet the church has moved out; a city mission is usually interdenominational and located in the downtown district where both good and bad people congregate nightly.

The City Rescue Mission of Grand Rapids—later called the Mel Trotter Mission and today identified as Mel Trotter Ministries—is a combination of an inner-city mission, a family mission, and a city mission. Homeless or transient people, some of whom are alcoholics and drug addicts, frequent it.

Mel Trotter Ministries helps those who are discouraged, sick, and in trouble. But it helps, too, those who come seeking the assurance of salvation. The testimonies and reminiscences placed between the chapters of this book tell the stories of all kinds of people who have come to the Mission. Some names have been changed to protect the privacy of individuals.

Mel Trotter Ministries' first and main objective is the salvation of the lost through the preaching and teaching of the gospel of Christ. Its second objective is to build Christian character, and its third objective is to alleviate human suffering by aiding the needy, whether with a bath, clean clothes, a warm meal, or a clean bed.

This ministry functions twenty-four hours a day, 365 days a year. While some churches contribute regularly, the Ministries' major support comes from generous-hearted and concerned individuals.

During the days of Mel Trotter, a branch Mission was started in southwest Grand Rapids. Today that branch is known as the Galewood Chapel. Through the years, hundreds of people were saved in that chapel, and many of them have gone into full-time Christian service. Recently, Mel Trotter Ministries expanded its outreach by building new quarters adjacent to the main Mission that houses homeless mothers with families.

From its inception in 1900 and now into the new millennium, the purpose of Mel Trotter Ministries has been and continues to be to serve the spiritual needs of the community. Thus, those who are associated with the Mission are and will always remain, in the words of Mel Trotter, "everlastingly at it!"

CHAPTER ONE

In the Beginning

MELVIN E. TROTTER was born on May 16, 1870, in Orangeville, Illinois. When Mel, one of seven children, was five years old, the family moved to Polo, Illinois, located in the center of a farming area.

Mel's father, William Trotter, tended bar, drinking as much as he served. William's wife, Emily, stayed at home and prayed. Such was the home and the life of Mel Trotter.

Mel's parents wanted him to get an education, but that wasn't what Mel had in mind. He liked spending time at his father's saloon and at the gambling den down the street. Mel, it seems, was following in the footsteps of his father.

In 1887 the family moved to Freeport, Illinois, where, at the age of seventeen, young Mel learned barbering. As soon as he began to draw a good salary, he left home. By the age of nineteen, he was drinking heavily and betting on "sure shots" until he finally lost his job.

Mel moved to Pearl City, Iowa, determined to continue in his trade. He thought that a new environment might help him. There, Mel met a wonderful Christian girl named Lottie Fisher. Soon after their marriage on April 23, 1891, Lottie received two big shocks—first, that her husband was an alcoholic, and second, that he had lost his job. Although Lottie and her friends did their

best to help Mel, his every attempt to reform ended in
failure.

When Mel lost his job in Pearl City, he and Lottie
moved to a rural area to get away from saloons and gambling. "I would have given my life to have stayed sober,"
said Mel. "I loathed the life I was living. I tried my level
best, but it wasn't in me."

Inside Mel raged a fiery craving, and, despite his wife's
pleadings, he couldn't stay sober. He fell into gambling,
lost yet another job, and moved on to Davenport, Iowa,
to try insurance work. In Davenport, Mel managed to
stay sober for eleven weeks. Then the craving for liquor
won out. He sold his horse for drinks and hit the saloons again.

For six years, Mel tried to quit. But every time he tried
to lift himself up, he fell—and then hated himself that
much more. He lost his insurance job the day after his
son was born.

Having a baby, though, was a wake-up call to Mel. He
knew that he had to give up his constant rounds of drinking and gambling. "I'll quit," he promised. And then he
promised again, and yet again. Perhaps the sight of his
child reminded him of his failure as a father. For whatever reason, Mel began to stay away from home—first a
few days at a time, then a week, and gradually longer
and longer.

One day, when his baby was about two years old, Mel
returned home after a ten-day period of drunkenness.
He found the baby dead in Lottie's arms. Mel felt like a
murderer. If only he hadn't spent all of their money on
drink, if only he'd been home when their baby had become sick, if only . . .

Suicide entered Mel's mind, but he didn't have the
courage.

As Mel stood beside the tiny white casket, he put his
arms around his wife. "I swear I'll never touch liquor

again as long as I live," he said. Two hours after the funeral, he staggered home so drunk he couldn't see.

Blaming himself for his child's death, Mel drank more and more in an effort to escape the guilt that flooded his soul. Following that awful day when he found his son dead, one continuous thought haunted him: he had murdered.

Mel hopped a freight car, and on January 19, 1897, the train rolled into the yards in Chicago during a bitter winter snowstorm. He dragged himself along the streets and, penniless, sold his shoes to get a drink. (This incident may be the origin of a false story of Mel taking the shoes off his baby in the coffin to sell them for a drink.)

When even that money ran out, Mel was kicked out of a Clark Street saloon. Dead drunk, broke, shoeless, and with almost no clothes on his back, Mel staggered along the street. People passed him by. No one cared, and Mel thought, *Who can blame them. I'm so dirt-begrimed that I disgust even myself.* At twenty-seven years of age, Mel Trotter was in utter despair. *Perhaps tonight I should end it all,* he thought. He directed his steps toward Lake Michigan.

But Mel's wife and his mother had never ceased praying—they cared! And God cared! Mel's path was directed to pass the Pacific Garden Mission. Tom Mackey, an ex-jockey and card shark, stood outside the Mission that night. He spotted the ragged bum on his way to the lake. He nudged Trotter inside and helped him find a seat against the wall.

On the platform was Harry Monroe, superintendent of the Mission. Monroe spotted Mel at the back of the room and stopped to ask the crowd to bow in prayer. "Oh, God, save that poor, poor boy," was his plea.

Monroe then gave his own testimony. In 1880 at the age of twenty-seven, Monroe explained, he had been saved after he wandered into the Mission. Although Mel was asleep for most of the service, he heard enough to realize that God had the power to heal and release him. So when Harry Monroe explained to Mel the way of salvation, Mel committed himself to the Lord Jesus Christ as his only hope. And God saved him, breaking the fetters that bound him. From that day, Mel never touched another drop of liquor, and he never wanted to do so.

Mel found a job barbering and soon was able to send for Lottie. They had only one room, but they were the happiest couple alive. "It is much better to live in one room and have Mel sober," said Lottie, "than live in a palace with a drunkard."

Mel wrote his mother about his conversion, and when she received the wonderful news, she fell to her knees and cried, "Thank God!" She had never stopped praying for him.

"My mother's prayers always followed me," said Mel, "even when I was in the worst condition. I never got so drunk or so far away that I could not always feel the hand of my mother."

Mel became known as "the man who raved about Jesus." And soon he would have ample opportunity to do just that.

The City Gets a Mission

ON DECEMBER 21, 1899, a committee of women and some local businessmen met in Grand Rapids, Michigan. These men and women were already sponsoring a small mission on Ellsworth Avenue. Their efforts had met with some success, and as a result a motion was made at this particular board meeting to extend mission work in Grand Rapids.

They had in mind to place the new mission on Canal Street. In 1899, four trolley car tracks and much liquor ran down Canal Street. Men and women of all ages and kinds frequented the many saloons as well as the old opera house, a building that boasted a bad reputation. The houses in this section were the oldest and most dilapidated in the city. Many of them had been moved from the better portions of town and placed along the riverfront. Nowhere else could such old, worn-out structures find tenants.

Such was the ramshackle red-light district that was eating at the vitals of Grand Rapids when the far-sighted Christian men and women of the committee saw the need of a mission. They voted to create a governing board and to appoint a missionary to supervise the work.

W. D. Patton, a founding member of the committee, gave an enthusiastic account of the work of the Pacific Garden Mission in Chicago. He suggested that Harry

Monroe, the superintendent of that Mission, be invited
to meet with them in the near future. Perhaps he could
bring some converts to conduct services and arouse
public interest in the establishment of a city rescue mission for Grand Rapids.

The committee contacted Monroe, and on February 2,
1900, Monroe arrived in Grand Rapids, accompanied by
four ex-drunkards, bums, and gamblers—among them
Melvin E. Trotter.

On Sunday afternoon and evening, they went to
Lockerby Hall, an old auditorium at Ionia and Foun-
tain Streets. M. B. Van Vranken, secretary of the Young
Men's Christian Association (YMCA), told the audience
that a group of local men and women were interested
in a rescue mission for Grand Rapids. Then and there
the committee voted to start one, and they raised one
thousand dollars as seed money.

The committee asked Mel Trotter to stay over an ex-
tra day. "We wonder," they asked, "if you would consider
the position of superintendent for our new mission?"

Mel Trotter had never led a mission meeting in his
life, but three weeks later, he become the superintendent of the City Rescue Mission. The beginnings were
humble—a dingy room in a vacant store at 95 Canal
Street (now lower Monroe Avenue). There the first
meeting of the City Rescue Mission was held.

The Lord blessed the work, and the very first night
there were conversions. Jerry, a policeman, was on duty
that night. "You never saw so many folks trying to get
in one little building," he said. "When Mel finally came
up from the old Eagle Hotel and found more women
there than men, he was scared stiff. He had never
worked with women, and you should have heard their
language. He got up and told them what he was there
for, told it in slang, and he didn't seem to know he was
using it. It was just the most natural thing in the world."

This was something new to Grand Rapids—a preacher who spoke the language of the streets! When Mel gave the invitation to come to Jesus, three young women responded. One of those young women went on to become a missionary, another one married a preacher, and the third one was associated with the Mission for many years.

"I can't tell you what a funny feeling I had during and after that meeting," said Jerry. "I said, 'Jesus is running this thing, and, believe me, He has been running it ever since.'"

But the work of the Mission was not without opposition. Every night a group of young men disrupted the meeting by laughing and singing dirty words to the hymns. Mel Trotter responded by introducing "muscular Christianity." He would start the group singing "More About Jesus," then he would grab a troublemaker and put him into the street. Mel put his brother George, a husky young man, at the door. With one Trotter in front and the other at the back, it was not a wise idea to start anything. God's work would be done regardless of hooligans.

It's a hard fact of life, however, that God's work requires money. When the money started to give out, the struggle to keep the doors open began. No one believed that a mission could succeed in so small a town as Grand Rapids. Folks said that it was perfectly all right in Chicago or New York, but Grand Rapids, Michigan?

"It won't last," they said.

"Only excitement!"

"Just a flash in the pan!"

"They will all get drunk again!"

"The crowds will quit coming!"

Yet, during all of this time the streets of Grand Rapids were filled with men and women who were unchurched and without Christ. When Trotter announced

that the Mission had "no law but love, and no creed but
Christ" and talked of Christ's ability to redeem men and
women, great crowds of people began to flock in. Then
the churches of Grand Rapids saw the purpose of the
Mission—it was there only to glorify God. When reports
of redeemed lives filtered out of the Mission, the
churches threw their support behind it.

Only a few weeks after the Mission opened, someone
brought Herb Sillaway, an alcoholic barber. The Ole'
Man—the nickname that the regulars gave to Mel
Trotter—was interested in barbers. He was one himself.
After Sillaway had been drunk for four days, Mel
straightened him up, got his job back, and gave him
some of his own barber tools to go to work.

Yet Sillaway got drunk six times in four weeks and
twice tried to commit suicide, the second time trying
to drown himself. He was fished out of the water in time,
however, and was taken to jail in his wet clothes with no
covering. The next morning Mel found him in a cell,
nearly dead. Herb's clothes were shriveled, and he was
trembling. Mel couldn't get any words out. He just stood
there and wept. Sillaway grabbed the bars and said, "My
God, man, I believe you love me."

"Yes, Herb," said Mel, "I love you like I love my own
soul."

Herb said, "You will never be ashamed of me again."

And Sillaway was as good as his word. He eventually
became Mel's assistant.

From Hellhole to Haven

MEL CALLED DR. DAVIS, pastor of the local presbyterian church, at two o'clock in the morning. A young woman had taken carbolic acid. She was on the verge of death and wanted to be baptized. Mel was constantly calling on the ministers in the city to baptize, marry, and do things that he, as a layman, was unable to do.

After that baptism ceremony, Dr. Davis said, "Why don't you become ordained?"

Mel had never thought of such a thing. Then Dr. Davis explained, "We can ordain you as an evangelist, and it will carry the privileges of an ordained minister."

When Mel went before the presbytery, however, he found out that being ordained as an evangelist did not carry the privilege of baptizing, marrying, or performing other ministerial duties. One of the ministers suggested that they ordain him as a minister. This appealed to the other men, and at once three or four were on their feet saying, "Let's do it now."

"Your examination," said one of the presbyters, "starts with Christian evidences."

Mel said, "What's that?"

They said, "Are you saved?"

Mel answered, "You bet!"

They said, "How do you know?"

Mel replied, "I was there when it happened, in the

Pacific Garden Mission, January 19, 1897, ten minutes
past nine, central time, Chicago, Illinois, U.S.A."

They all laughed. Then they asked him what he knew
about church history.

Mel said, "You know more about that than I do."

Then he was asked, "Are you Calvinistic or Arminian?"

Mel said, "My father is Irish."

When they asked him about his doctrine, he told
them, "It is the Monroe doctrine. Harry Monroe taught
me everything I know."

Dr. French was one of Mel's questioners that day. He
was a marvelous old minister but a real stickler for
church law. When the motion was made to ordain Mel,
Dr. French slowly rose to his feet. "Gentlemen," he said,
"you realize these proceedings establish an unorthodox
precedent." Everyone was silent. "Well," Dr. French continued, "find us another Mel Trotter, and we will ordain
him, too! I second the motion!"

In 1905, in just seven minutes, Mel became an ordained Presbyterian minister.

Dr. French had added a postscript to the proceedings
of that day. "Who are we to refuse ordination to one
whom God has ordained? God has put His hand on this
man."

If the growth of the City Rescue Mission was any in-
dicator, Dr. French was on the right track. A few months
after Mel Trotter became superintendent, a mighty revival broke out, and every night there were from two to
twenty-five souls who found the Lord. These converts
included old drunken Jack Krouskopf and his wife Anna;
Sillaway, the drunken barber; Colgrove, who became a
successful evangelist; Dad Keough, an old rounder who
had been around the world seven times; and George
Trotter, Mel's brother. All of them were saved about the
same time. In fact, there were fifteen hundred conversions that first year.

Why such phenomenal numbers? Perhaps Grand Rapids was just ready for a revival. Or maybe it was because when Mel Trotter preached the gospel, he spoke the language of the street people. Or it could be that the down-and-outs, when they heard about Mel Trotter's unsavory past, knew that he spoke to them from his heart. Whatever the reason, there was no doubt that God was working through the Mission.

As the crowds all but pushed the walls out at the Canal Street location, it became obvious that the Mission needed more room. A site was found on Market Street and a one-story building was constructed in forty-four days. To finance construction, five men gave five hundred dollars each, and the rest was raised by selling bricks at ten cents apiece.

At the Market Street location, which held 750 chairs, Mel Trotter had the finest Mission in the country. But almost at once it was packed to the doors. Often people were standing in the street. They just kept getting saved and joining the church.

In two years, a two-story addition was built, thus giving them a thousand chairs. By that time, Sunday school attendance was up to two hundred. Special classes for beginners, personal workers, and men were also held. And on Sunday nights the crowds kept growing. Hundreds were turned away for lack of room. Then one day in the noon prayer meeting, the men and women looked from the south window of the Mission, and, with nothing in their pockets but with faith in their hearts, they claimed the Smith Opera House for God.

Smith's was then the center of the old "tenderloin" district, and the home of unspeakable moral corruption. In its heyday, the opera house had been one of the most handsome buildings in the city. The auditorium could seat eleven hundred people, and eight private boxes were festooned with silk and lace. But during its later years the theater became known as "the wicked old Smith Opera House." Those curtained boxes hid every form of possible sin. Burlesque replaced legitimate theater, and drinks were hawked up and down the aisles between acts. The four club rooms upstairs were used for purposes far different from those originally intended.

But Mel Trotter had a vision for the forlorn building. In his mind's eye he could see those eleven hundred seats filled by those who were being turned away at the Mission. The meeting rooms upstairs would hold sessions of the S. S. Society—the Soul Seekers—whose motto was "Saved to Serve" and who supported a missionary in India.

Those rooms could also hold the 250 children enrolled in the Mission's Sunday school program. There would be room for the Mothers' Meetings, those dedicated women who had collected and sewn garments for more than two hundred needy families that year. Mel could visualize a hundred men and women seated in another part of the old opera house, searching the Scriptures in the adult Bible class.

For some time, too, Mel had been concerned about the young girls who came to the city looking for work. They faced temptations and dangers, and with enough space the Mission could provide an uplifting and safe haven. And for those young women who got "in trouble," an enlarged Mission would offer help, shelter, and an escape from back-alley abortionists.

Yes, the wicked old opera house could be redeemed and could witness the redemption of many lost souls within its walls. But where would they find the money? At the end of 1903, the treasury held a balance of $7.95. The purchase price for the Smith Opera House was forty-seven thousand dollars!

That Mel Trotter possessed a certain amount of showmanship when he preached old-fashioned hellfire and brimstone cannot be denied. But he had placed complete trust in God to meet the needs of his Mission. And God came through.

Decker and Jean Realtors, local real estate dealers, secured a sixty-day option for five thousand dollars on the old opera house. The owners never dreamed that the balance could be paid in so short a time. Figuring that they were five thousand dollars to the good, they contracted with Empire, a theatrical company, for the next four years. To their surprise, consternation, and dismay, before the expiration of the option, the balance of the agreed purchase price was paid!

Then commenced a big struggle for possession. First, Empire asked the city council for a new license to conduct theatricals in the old place. This was promptly turned down through the intervention of the mayor of Grand Rapids.

Then Empire tried to take forcible possession. When "Cherry Blossoms," the first production under the new contract, came to town, Trotter was at Winona Lake, Indiana. On Saturday night, he was notified that Empire was about to take possession. All of the trains had gone, except the Limited, which did not stop. In desperation, Mel wired his friend, Dr. Scott, secretary to the president of the Pennsylvania Railway. The Limited made a special stop at Winona Lake that night, and by five o'clock Sunday morning all of the doors of the opera house were barred, and armed men stood guard inside.

Next, someone attempted unsuccessfully to set fire to the opera house. Then Mel Trotter received threats on his life. But he was sure that God had given him the order to buy, and he remained committed.

In 1906, the news broke upon the city that Mel Trotter had taken over the Smith Opera House. Decker and

Jean Realtors took out an option, and the donations poured in. The opera house was formally opened as a Mission on September 20, 1907. While the official ceremonies proceeded upstairs, Trotter went down into the basement and wept.

CHAPTER FOUR

To Save unto the Uttermost

THE BUILDING THAT ONCE echoed with laughter from bawdy revelers now chimed with the voices of children singing "Jesus Loves Me." The Mission's Sunday school served children from all parts of the city, with an average attendance of about 360 to five hundred. They met at three o'clock in the afternoon, so as not to conflict with other schools, most of which met in the morning.

Many of the children had received help from the Mission in the form of clothing, food, and household items. People who saw the students and were impressed with their respectable appearance knew little about the work invested to produce such results.

By 1913, the Sunday school had thirty-five teachers, all of whom had accepted Christ as Savior before they were entrusted with a class of children. The Sunday school held as many as forty-five "decision days," and to bring children to Christ, the teachers had to be qualified to lead. So preceding decision days, the teachers met for prayer, entrusting the class and the message to the Spirit of God. During class on decision days, regular lessons were suspended and time was spent in explaining the plan of salvation in the simplest possible way. The teachers did not play on the emotions of the children. Instead, the Spirit of God was allowed to do the work. Consequently, many of the teachers reported, "All the scholars in my class are won for Christ."

And the children's faith was sincere. They were interested not only in attending their own classes but also in contributing to the work of the Mission. One year they pledged four hundred dollars to the Mission's funds— and paid it.

The Sunday school program sometimes reaped other unexpected results. One mother brought her child to class for the first time. She sat in the room and listened to the little ones sing "Jesus loves me, this I know." Her heart was touched, and she realized how much she needed a Savior. That night she came to the Mission and was among the first to respond to the invitation to come to Christ.

And as the little ones sang, the Mission buzzed with activity—men, women, and young people either working, studying, singing, or attending meetings. The first order of work was the building itself. Someone was always sweeping, scrubbing, or polishing, keeping the building clean and sanitary despite its constant use— twenty-four hours a day, 365 days a year.

By 1913, the City Rescue Mission held twenty-three meetings every week. In addition to the nightly evangelistic services, as well as special music and singing, the Mission held a variety of groups and classes. Every Friday there was a Bible class with an average of sixteen-hundred members. A men's Bible class met every Tuesday night, and a women's Bible class met on Sunday afternoon. A Soul Seekers' Class of more than fifty young women met on Friday nights, and the Mothers' Meeting met on Wednesday afternoons to sew for the poor. Then there was a Friday afternoon women's prayer meeting, and a men and women's prayer meeting on Saturday nights.

The Young People's Society met on Sunday afternoons. They held discussions and invited their friends, seeking to bring them into a personal acquaintance with Jesus Christ. This group of young people also contributed financially to the work of the Mission, one year giving fifty dollars.

Street meetings were another outreach service, and in that work the Mission used the "gospel truck." Every night workers went into the streets to preach the gospel to the great numbers of people who never came into the Mission or went to a church. At each of these services, men and women were given an opportunity to accept Christ, and the Word of God was placed into their hands. Sometimes people followed the truck to the Mission, where they surrendered themselves to Christ.

In addition to the regular day-to-day work at the Mission there were three annual special occasions: Thanksgiving, when food baskets and children's clothing were given to poor families; Christmas, when, in addition to providing food and clothing, the Mission hosted a Christmas tree program; and the Mission picnic in July at Jenison Park. This picnic was often the only vacation that tired mothers had during the year.

The years of work had given the City Rescue Mission the opportunity to know the city and its problems. And although the Mission had a heart for helping people, every effort ultimately had in view the conversion of people to Christ. Through the outreach missions of City Rescue Mission, many stories of human redemption were enacted.

. . . I was in prison, and you came to Me . . .

Rev. C. R. Roadarmel served as jail outreach minister during 1913. He attended the police court every morning, after which he conducted personal work at the county jail. Through the jail ministry program, the Mission acted in conjunction with judges in the cases that seemed most hopeful.

The police court judges thought that the Mission was of special value in the probation work of the court and in dealing with persons on parole. When prisoners volunteered to work with the Mission, the judges felt that those men were on the road to reformation. Many released prisoners reported that, by associating with the Rescue Mission, they received valuable assistance in living up to the conditions of probation.

Mark was sent to jail for eighty days in April 1912, for nonsupport of his family. Drink had gotten a grip of him, holding him like a slave. When Mark's wife, Janet, went to the judge to ask whether anything could be done for her husband, the judge sent her to the Rescue Mission. After hearing Janet's story, a jail minister went to Mark.

"All of my friends had abandoned me," said Mark, "and I guess I was ready to hear the gospel. But the Good News seemed too good to be true. Could it be possible that Jesus could care for me when the world had cast me off? I went back to my cell and wept like a child. The love of Jesus broke my heart."

The minister came back to the jail with a one hundred dollar bond signed by Mel Trotter, which enabled Mark to be released to the Mission.

"I had never been there before," Mark said, "except when it was the old Smith Opera House."

Since Mark had no money, Mel gave him a silver dollar. Then Mark attended the half past seven evening meeting, where he gave his heart to God. Janet went to the altar with him, and they began to serve the Lord together.

"It was no easy matter to rise above the ruin I had brought to my family. My home was gone, and I'd lost my job as switchman on the railroad. But when the yard master found out I had resolved to lead a straight life, he got me my job back.

"I often get a bunch of my mates together and tell them what wonderful things God has done for me. I believe that God will bless my testimony to the salvation of those who work with me. Some of them need, as much as I did, to know what Jesus Christ can do in a man's life."

Not all prisoners were allowed, like Mark, to get out on bond. But even if a man was denied probation, the jail ministry still proved fruitful. The Rev. Roadarmel visited a young farmer named Jim. Jim was about twenty-seven years of age, and he was serving forty-five days for stealing a skunk hide. "That is a very stinking and offensive crime," said Rev. Roadarmel. Soon, though, Jim began thinking seriously about the gospel and was led to the Savior. A few days later, Jim was out cleaning sidewalks around the jail. His decision to trust in Christ led to his becoming a trustee at the jail.

Although Rev. Roadarmel sometimes had to convince a prisoner to talk to him, one young man in jail, Ted, actually sent for him. Ted hadn't been home in years, and he wanted to begin a Christian life. The minister called the young man's mother. She came, arranged for his release, and took him home.

It was not always men who ended up in jail. An eighteen-year-old girl named Nell got into trouble after her mother's death. She would throw her clothes out of the window after dark and later sneak out to a shed to dress. Then she would spend the night walking the streets. One night, her father caught her coming in and told her that his home was no longer hers. Three days later, Rev. Roadarmel found her in the police court. She had been arrested in a coal yard. She had spent one night at the home of a girlfriend, another in an outdoor toilet, and the last in a coal shed. When Nell arrived at police headquarters, the matron scrubbed her for nearly an hour.

The judge turned Nell over to the Mission. Miss Hanink, a Mission worker, took Nell in hand, clothed her, and loved her. Nell soon professed faith in Christ and returned home.

The Mission jail ministry never turned down a single case in which a judge sought its help and interest. No matter how bad the case, even if it had been handled before without success and with great disappointment, the ministry was always ready to take it up again and give the man or woman another chance.

. . . I was sick, and you visited Me . . .

Rev. Roadarmel also visited the hospitals every afternoon. "Many people," he said, "never think of God, it seems, until they are sick. One fine lad, Tommy, aged sixteen, was there with a foot that had been crushed in an elevator. His Christian parents and pastor had not taught him about personal acceptance of Christ. I found him without Christ, but though he was still in pain, I left him happy in Jesus."

In one of the hospitals a young man named Edward called Rev. Roadarmel to his bed and asked him to pray for him. Edward then prayed for himself and, in a very reasoned way, accepted the finished work of Christ. After his discharge from the hospital, Edward said, "Before I got sick I never had time to think of matters of the soul. Thank God for my sickness."

Another outreach program involved home visits. One home visitor climbed a set of rickety stairs to find a family living in one room. The mother was haggard and discouraged, the children barefooted. The rent was a month overdue, there was no food in the house, and even the blankets were not paid for. The Mission supplied their immediate needs with food and clothing.

In another home the conditions were so distressful because of the mother's illness that the home visitor set to work and cleaned things up. The Mission then sent beds, mattresses, springs, and bedding to the house along with a basket of provisions—all that was necessary for the family's immediate needs. The ultimate object of the Rescue Mission, of course, was to win this family to Christ.

. . . I was naked and you clothed Me . . .

The clothes room helped the Mission reach many needy people in the community. On a cold, stormy day, a great number of women and children would be waiting just outside the clothes room. The Mission workers talked with them, prayed with them, and then fitted them out with the necessary clothing.

The men came for clothing, too. One man was taken to the clothes room and told about the Lord. Then he was given a new set of clothes. The next day, he came back with his wife.

"Did you give him these clothes?" she asked.

"Yes," said a worker. "We gave them to him."

"I thought he had stolen them," the wife said as she heaved a sign of relief. "They are better than any he has ever had since we were married."

Lottie Trotter, along with several helpers, was most often found in the clothes room. A glance at the well-stocked shelves showed both new and used clothing. The women made sure there were no buttonless garments in the Rescue Mission clothes room. Clothing store proprietors often sent supplies of new garments such as coats, sweaters, stockings, gloves, and shoes of different sizes. Donations were always welcome.

But there were hand-sewn garments as well. Women in comfortable circumstances, but who were glad to be associated with the Mission, came together in Mothers' Meetings to make garments for their poorer sisters. And less fortunate women contributed, too, through the Martha Mission Circle.

Lottie Trotter holds that the idea for the Martha Mission was directly God-given. She had for some time felt a burden about women who had no idea of how to sew and consequently were unable to teach their daughters. She was so burdened that she woke one night, pondering and praying about the best way to reach them. The whole plan came to her, down to the smallest detail. When she had seen the pattern that God showed her, she fell asleep again, then woke to carry it out.

Instead of always bringing the mothers to the Mission, Lottie instituted the practice of holding the Martha Mission Circle in the mothers' own homes. She took bags containing fabric and notions to the circle meetings, and the women learned, though late in life, to cut and sew.

"Just look," one of the Circle members would say, holding up a pillowcase. "I made this all myself." Another would display a tiny shirt. "I made this for my baby!"

Nothing like the Martha's Circle had been tried through any known mission outreach, and so successful did it prove that it was regarded as the most fruitful enterprise of its kind. But pillowcases and baby shirts were not the only fruit of this labor. It also elevated the home life of the women. When the time came for a woman to receive the Circle at her house, she scrubbed and cleaned and polished as never before. "Mrs. Smith made her home look spotlessly clean when we were there a week ago," Mrs. Jones would say. "Mine must be as free from dust and dirt as hers."

Visiting other homes also brought out compassion in the women. "I thought my lot was the hardest of all the mothers," said a Martha member, "but poor as we are, there are many in a worse position."

Still, the ultimate goal of the Martha Mission Circle was winning souls to Christ. After the sewing time came a Bible lesson. Lottie's face literally beamed with joy as she told of the spiritual fruit of this work.

"Many of these women," said Lottie, "had not been in a religious meeting for years until we followed them into their homes and carried the message of salvation to them there. Within six months we have had over twenty conversions among these women. They are so interested that it is the hardest thing to keep them away from the meetings of the Martha Mission Circle."

All of the Mission's weekly meetings and every ministry and program was supported totally by private freewill offerings. Considering the many appeals to the public for money from various worthy causes, one naturally asks, "Why this generosity to the City Rescue Mission?" It certainly demonstrated confidence in the superintendent and his wife, the workers, the management, and the work.

The work, of course, was rescuing lost souls. But the Mission first rescued lost lives, and that work began with the question, "Can we by any means make a man or woman out of you?"

Many were the citizens of Grand Rapids who heartily agreed that there was no more valuable work than that of the Mission. Mr. Stanton, owner of a business in the Mission district, said, "A vast improvement has taken place in the district where the Mission operates. Many saloons and houses of ill-fame have been closed; the value of property has increased enormously."

But far exceeding the immediate benefits of the Mission were the dividends reaped in reclaimed lives. When men and women came to Christ, they not only repaired their own lives but also ceased to damage the lives of loved ones. That untold damage can never be calculated. A clerk who worked at the Mission said, "If the public only knew all we know, they would appreciate our work here even more."

Of course not every story of the Mission had a happy outcome. There were times of heartbreak and discouragement, yet everyone associated with the City Rescue Mission considered it a privilege to do the work that God had given them—to save unto the uttermost.

> *"Inasmuch as ye have done it unto one of the least*
> *of these my brethren, ye have done it unto me."*
>   (Matt. 25:40 KJV)

A House of Power

THERE WERE NOT MANY places of worship in Grand Rapids where people begged to enter. But on Sunday nights people crowded around the entrance of the City Rescue Mission and pleaded to get in.

"My husband is sick, and I haven't been able to get here all week," a woman was heard to say, "and now that I have come, there are so many people I can't get in!"

What drew so many people to the Rescue Mission? What was its power?

First, the Mission served to keep alive the realities of the Christian faith. Its purpose was to apply the principles of the Sermon on the Mount and the workings of the gospel of Christ to the individual. The beliefs of the Mission are best expressed by the motto that hung on the walls of the Mission: "No creed but Christ; no law but love."

Everyone who went into the Rescue Mission heard the testimonies of those who had come under the uplifting and regenerating power of the gospel. Converts related their testimonies honestly and simply. Those who listened could not help but feel that they had come up against reality.

Every person is hungry for a religion that fills his or her soul in the same way that the love of a spouse or children fills it. That can be accomplished only by the most elementary views of God and His Son, Jesus Christ.

The higher critics have their place. But the elementary view of the great truths is what drew people into the Mission. Poor, forlorn, down-and-out men and women went there, heard the message, listened to the testimonies, and came out living men and women.

Second, the Rescue Mission and its work served as a religious laboratory. Experimental religion was being illustrated constantly in ministries such as the Martha Mission Circle and the gospel truck. Through the Mission and its ministries, the whole community found fresh testimony that, one at a time, miracles happened.

Soul-touching testimonies, ministries that lived the kingdom of God, innovative programs—all contributed to the success of the Mission. But every person associated with the Mission would have agreed that the Saturday night prayer and praise meetings were, to a large extent, responsible for injecting power into the City Rescue Mission. And everyone would have pointed particularly to the men's prayer meeting—which was held in the dark! With bowed heads, sitting and kneeling together in darkness, the men were safe from all distractions and disturbances. They couldn't even see one another.

Sometimes all the men prayed aloud, yet there was no confusion. And when a supplicant laid hold upon God, the very atmosphere seemed charged with spiritual power. Then, filled with heavenly joy, the men laughed and cried and responded. Workers in the office would come to the door to catch from without something of the holy fire that was burning within.

When the lights were turned up, everyone sang choruses, and it seemed as if they could go on all night. Trotter led the singing and declared that he was in no hurry to go home, although it was often rapidly approaching midnight. With hands uplifted, hearts burning, and faces shining with the "light that never shone on sea or shore," the men sang:

The Spirit answers to the Blood
And tells me I am born of God.
Before the throng my surety stands,
My name is written on His hands.

The half cannot be fancied
This side the golden shore,
But there He'll be far sweeter
Than He ever was before.

One cannot speak of the power of the City Rescue Mission without speaking of its superintendent, Mel Trotter. But certainly Mel would have denied that the power came from him.

It's true that many people considered Mel to be a civic asset, and indeed he became a Grand Rapids institution. Although deserving of the title of *Reverend,* he preferred plain Mel Trotter, or the Ole' Man.

But stronger than the respect Mel garnered from the community was his reverence for the Word of God and his wholehearted belief in its authority. He came to that reverence the hard way, and God was able to use him so effectively because he had been through the mill. No one can appeal to people who have hit bottom more successfully than one who has experienced the same depths.

Thus, Mel reached people no one else reached. The down-and-outs recognized at once that Mel had been down their road. They knew where he had begun, and when they recognized where he had ended, hope sprang up in hopeless lives. He demonstrated in his daily life the redemptive power of human helpfulness and Christian brotherhood. His work was his best argument.

Mel's unfortunate past was the basis of the remarkable tactfulness that was exhibited in the work of the Mission. Mel treated each individual with the tenderness

of a father, but he used the concept of tough love long
before the term was ever coined.

"There are children so wayward and stiff-necked," Mel
said, "that indulging their behavior would be the worst
possible course. There are not a few cases in rescue work,
as in the home, where to spare the rod is to spoil the child."

A final source of power for the Mission was the wise
and economical way that funds were expended. In fact,
for every $4.60 the Mission spent, there was a man or
woman praising God for salvation. The accounts of the
Mission were audited every month, and the books were
always found to be well kept. Every year they finished a
few dollars in the black. "The ease with which Mr. Trotter raises his annual requirements," said Mr. Stanton, a
business owner, "is a pretty good proof of our appreciation of the work."

Although Mr. Stanton's business was groceries, he
knew that there was no better investment than making
homes happy through sobriety, transforming criminals
into productive citizens, and lifting those people who
had fallen—all made possible because of lives redeemed
from destruction.

The City Rescue Mission saw a lot of down-and-out
men come through its doors, but the Mission history
includes stories of lost and wretched women as well.
Some old mission documents revealed the story of one
such woman.

Mike, a traffic cop, rushed to a young woman and
snatched the crying baby from her arms. "Are you hurt,
ma'am? Is the kid hurt? Didn't you see the traffic light?
The soft snow saved your life. Here, put your hat on,
ma'am—Sue, is that you? What are you doing out on such
a cold night? Are you drinkin' again? Why this baby's
cold, wet, and sick. I'll send her up to the station house
and you can get her in the morning."

"No, Mike, don't take her," Sue pleaded. "I'll never

get her back, and if I lose her, I'll die. I've lost everything else. Please, Mike. I'm not drinking much. I didn't
see the auto, honestly, I didn't. I'm all right."

Mike started for the station on foot, carrying the baby
in his arms. Sue walked a block with them, then she
kissed her baby goodnight and turned down the street.
In an hour, she had forgotten her baby, Mike, and everything else.

Sue had been the most popular girl in school, kind
to everyone and unselfish to a fault. After the sudden
death of her father, she had to quit school and work to
help support the family.

At work, many men were attracted to Sue, but there
was never anyone special. But when the company installed some modern machinery, a man named Fred
Adams came from the East to supervise the installation.
He was a fine-looking young fellow and very clever. The
moment he entered the door, Sue lost her head, and
Fred could see no one but Sue. In a short time, they
were married.

Fred liked his drink and soon learned that Sue was
at her best when she had a drink or two. The young
crowd called her the life of the party, and it wasn't long
before Sue felt it very necessary to have her drink.

While Fred sat in a saloon one afternoon, an officer
came in with a warrant for his arrest. Sue was utterly
destroyed to find out that Fred had a wife and a baby in
Boston. In a few weeks, Sue's child was to be born.

Still, Sue's beauty brought her new friends, and her
love for drink gradually led her to places she had never
expected to go. With her self-respect gone, she started
out one night for one of the old haunts, carrying her
baby on her arm. She was hit by an auto, and that's when
Mike found her. The next day, Sue left for Chicago, and
a fine family outside the city adopted the baby.

For months after that, Sue lived the "don't think—just

forget it" life, but an awful awakening came at last. It was the day before Christmas. Chicago's shopping district was a happy scene. Men and women were busy shopping. Children screamed with delight at Santa Claus. All seemed happy and carefree.

As Sue entered a department store through the revolving door, a lovely baby girl about two and a half years old looked up at her and said, "See baby's dolly." Sue's whole awful failure flooded her soul until she cried aloud in her agony, "My God, is she dead? Have I murdered my baby? Maybe she is yet alive. Oh, God, help me. I'll go home and find her."

With fifty cents in her purse, Sue pawned her only ring and caught the first train to Michigan. Through the work of Providence, Sue found herself in front of the City Rescue Mission. The doorway was crowded, but, drawn by the powerful spiritual energy from within, Sue worked her way through. There on the stage was a Christmas tree and all that goes with it—a real Santa Claus and presents for everyone.

After a song by the congregation and Sunday school children, the superintendent—someone called him the Ole' Man—stepped to the front of the stage and told the true meaning of Christmas; how it was the birthday of Jesus; how He was born to Mary; how He grew and did good; and how at last He died to make us good.

Sue listened and relived her childhood all over again. She knew that story by heart but had forgotten it in her sorrow and trouble.

The program went on with more or less confusion—dialogues, songs, and class recitations. The last number was to be a song by a little fellow who was badly deformed. His shoulders were as high as his head, and he had a large hump on his back. After his name was called, Jack came to the platform.

As he came to the center of the platform, a teenager

yelled out, "Hello, Hump! Is that your Santa Claus pack on your back?"

Jack turned as pale as a ghost, and then as red as a beet. He began to cry, but he didn't leave the platform. He stood there and sobbed as if his heart would break. "I can't help it! I can't help it!"

Then, out of the crowd a man rushed to him, took him in his arms, and said, "Don't cry, Jack. Yer the finest boy in this school."

Then turning to the crowd, the man, still holding the boy, said, "I'm Bill, and this is my son, Jack. It's not the boy's fault he's like this. Old booze is to blame. I came home one night in the old days and found the door locked. I pounded it with my fist. My wife, with little Jack here on her arm, came to the door as fast as she could. There was no food in the house, and she tried to nurse a baby when she had no nourishment for herself.

"When she opened the door, I grabbed her wrist; and before she realized what I was doing, she and baby Jack had gone headlong down the stairs. And that's why our little Jack is like you see him."

The room was silent, and after a great effort Bill continued. "Folks from this Mission came to our help. They brought things to eat and helped care for Jack while he was so sick. I was brokenhearted over my baby—blamed myself—and I refused to go to the Mission. I wouldn't even let them talk to me. At last, I left my family and stayed drunk until I was arrested."

Bill swallowed and continued. "A Sunday morning crowd from the Mission came to jail for a service. I refused to come out of my cell. The singing was good, but I played cards with another man. Then a little thin voice sang, 'Jesus bids us shine.' It was baby Jack's voice. My God, how sweetly he can sing. I dropped my cards, crawled into my bunk, and covered my head. Finally, the man who had charge of the meeting brought Jack to my cell, and Jack called for his daddy. That settled it. Then and there I gave my heart to God, and never a drink since."

Sue bolted from her place and rushed to the door-keeper. She asked if she could talk to the man who had just spoken. That night Bill told Sue all about the one answer to her heartache—to trust in the Lord Jesus Christ. And that very night, the best she knew how, Sue surrendered herself to God.

After a prayer, Bill took Sue by the hand, led her to a woman who had a kind face, and wished her Godspeed.

Everyone knew Sophie Boughner as just "Sophie of the Mission." She had been converted in the Mission some years before, after a life of many poor choices. She knew, like no one else could possibly know, just what Sue needed in her awful condition. Sophie took Sue home with her and cared for her; Sophie watched and prayed through the night while Sue slept.

The next day, they came to the Mission. Mel Trotter asked Sue, "What kind of work can you do?" She said, "I can sew."

Sue went to work as an assistant in the alteration department of a large department store. That gave her a chance to be at the Mission every night. It became her keenest delight to get hold of any girl who needed help. But after she and Sophie returned home at night, Sue's heart would ache for her baby. She wanted so much to see her.

Finally Sophie said to her, "I might as well tell you the truth. I have been through the same experience. I could not find rest or peace, and finally one day in desperation I went to Mr. Trotter. I asked him if God would let me have my baby in heaven. He said, 'Yes, He will.' I made up my mind that if God would do that, I would just live here and get everyone I met in touch with the

Lord Jesus Christ, and when I get to heaven, we will be a united family."

Sophie took Sue by the hand and said, "With that thought in mind, I went to work, with my heart and mind stayed on the things of God; and in His own good time He took care of everything. He will for you, too. I'm sure the day will come that, if God wants you to have your children back, He will give them to you."

While her mother's heart continued its longing, Sue gave herself entirely to the power of the Spirit, and she was healed by helping others.

In the June 1951 issue of the Mission newsletter, the following announcement appeared:

SOPHIA BOUGHNER (1876–1951)

Another one of God's dear servants has been called Home to her reward. Any person who for the last forty years has been in and around the Mel Trotter Mission will recall the smile and friendly greeting of dear old Sophie. "Pray much" was one of her favorite greetings, and she was never too busy or too tired to stop for a word of prayer with anyone who asked.

Almost fifty years ago, Sophia Boughner wandered into the old City Rescue Mission on a Christmas night, and for almost fifty years she worked for the Lord, winning souls to Him wherever she went, relieving the suffering of the poor and needy, ready to go one more step or perform one more act of love. As a personal worker, she was "everlastingly at it" with a sweet and winning manner.

On May 18, 1951, early in the morning, Sophie Boughner was ushered into the presence of the One she had chosen to serve so faithfully for so many years.

CHAPTER SIX

Saved to Serve

MEL TROTTER HAD HIS CRITICS. Some people said that his work was a personal thing, that the City Rescue Mission was becoming a one-man power enterprise. But that fear was soon put to rest as Mel Trotter began to groom understudies who could carry on his work when he was obliged to relinquish it.

With the success of the Mission work in a town the size of Grand Rapids, other smaller cities wanted missions. Mel began opening numbers of them throughout the United States, and men who had first received Christ in the Grand Rapids Mission were now leading missions in forty cities.

Mel was once asked, "What gives you the greatest satisfaction as you look back over the sixteen years since your conversion?" He replied without a moment of hesitation, "The wonderful lot of men standing for Christ and preaching the gospel. Nothing," he said, "gives me such joy as to know that if I never opened my lips tonight, forty doors would swing open, and forty men would lead a red-hot, soul-saving campaign in the other missions."

More than thirty thousand men and women were reported as seekers after salvation in those other missions during the year 1915. The men who superintended the work in those missions had begun their training at the Grand Rapids Mission. A janitor at the City Rescue

Mission, for instance, could someday become a super-intendent if he availed himself of every opportunity to qualify for a position of responsibility. When called to it, he could play the part without any difficulty. He could say, "If Trotter can do it, I can." And he would. That is the hope of this marvelous work—that those who were once lost in sin can become leaders, leading others to Christ.

Jack was one example of such hope fulfilled. He was one of the worst cases that ever came into the Mission. He had a six-weeks' growth of beard and for five years had never drawn a sober breath. At one time he had cleaned spittoons for a drink.

"I cannot tell you how I came to Grand Rapids," said Jack. "I had been arrested for drunkenness eight times since arriving in Grand Rapids. At police court they said, 'Go out and die, for you are not fit to live.'"

Somehow Jack found himself in one of the back seats in the City Rescue Mission. "Someone came to me and got me to the altar, and that night I gave myself to Christ. They had no beds, and they suggested I go out and seek one. I begged them not to put me out, for I was afraid the temptation of the saloon would be too strong for me. So they fixed a bed for me here.

"For three years I took busted men to the clothes room, fixed them up with clothes, and did my best to boost them.

"Last June I went to Cleveland to help in the Rescue Mission there. I worked at my trade as an art glass worker in the daytime and helped in the Mission in the evening."

The men at the glass works tempted Jack by putting whiskey on his table, hoping the smell of it would tempt him. The foreman told those men if they didn't leave Jack alone, he would fire them. Jack later searched out the man that had persecuted him the most and led him to Christ, along with his wife and four children.

The glassworks made Jack treasurer of the Labor Parade Fund. They said, "We've been watching you closely and have come to the conclusion we would rather trust you than anyone else in the shop."

Jack held a part-time position of responsibility in the Cleveland Mission at night, but other Grand Rapids converts held full-time Mission jobs. George Soerheide, for instance, was brought to the Mission by his brother Jeff. Jeff had said, "It's a great place, and there are some of the finest-looking girls down there you have ever seen."

The following Saturday night, George went to the Mission. He stayed for the prayer meeting, and all of the men went up into a little room, closed the door, turned out the lights, and went down on their knees. George sat up straight in a chair and wished he was somewhere else, but he could not get out.

Finally Bill Van Domelen crawled over on his knees, put his head on George's lap, and as he told George he could be a Christian, Van's hot tears burned their way onto George's leg. The Spirit of God got hold of George, and he got down on his knees. He was wonderfully saved.

"I spent every night in the Mission," said George, "and I met a good-looking girl. It was a case of love at first sight."

Not long afterward, George and Florence were married and took up their work together. They had a baby boy, and how that child brightened their lives. But in a short time, God took the baby up to be with Him.

George made up his mind that he would go out after other boys, and he was determined to start a Sunday school class. He told a couple of new boys, "You bring in about ten more boys, and we'll all have dinner at the Eagle Hotel next Thursday."

The kids brought George more boys than he had anticipated, but he never said a word. He fed them a big dinner, and when they finished, he leaned over the table and told those little fellows, "I want you all to meet me in the Mission next Sunday afternoon to form a Sunday school class." They all promised to be there and bring someone else along.

For the first few Sundays they almost tore the room apart. When they grew too noisy, George would talk about Ty Cobb's batting average and how he could steal second. Then George would say, "Now before I tell you how he stole home, I must give you the rest of this lesson."

When the boys began to squirm again, George would give them a little more baseball. And that class grew. You just couldn't keep the boys away.

All things work together for good to them that love God, to them who are called according to His purpose (see Rom. 8:28), and when Cleveland, Ohio, asked Mel Trotter to open a mission there, George went down to run it.

Art Blackmore was another example of a life redeemed. Art, a barber, was a fine man, an all-around good sport, but far away from God. His wife tried her best to live for God, but Art insisted that she go to places she didn't want to go. One Sunday night, he dragged her to a show that turned out to be racy. When they returned home, Mrs. Blackmore faced Art and said, "I'm through going to those places with you. If it takes that to keep our home together, it will have to break."

Art said, "I've been wondering how much religion you really had and how deeply it went. I've been wanting to be a Christian ever since I heard that gospel truck at the corner of Bridge and Canal Streets. I thought if it amounted to anything, you would show it. This is the thing I've been waiting for."

The next Sunday night, they came to the Mission, and

he responded to the first invitation. Soon, Art left his
barber shop and worked in the Mission. He was there
for a good many years.

Several cities wanted Art as their Mission superintendent, but Mel Trotter was away so much that Art was
needed in the home Mission. When a need arose in Erie,
Pennsylvania, though, Mel sent Art, and he served the
Lord there for many years.

And what a blessing the Blackmores had in their two
sons, Carl and Jack. Carl became a songwriter and
musician who composed many gospel songs, including
"Some Golden Daybreak." Jack became a successful
attorney.

Jack, George, and Art all had been traveling down a
similar road but, by the grace of God, took the turnoff
into the City Rescue Mission. They learned a new route
through life—the road of salvation. And they, along with
many other Mission converts, went on to show the way
to countless others, testifying in their belief that they
had been saved to serve.

Testimony of Sergeant Henry Getty

In 1912, I wanted to show my Christian mother and father that I could live my own life. From 1912 to 1915, I
lived a life of sin. I say this with tears in my eyes. I went
down into the depths of sin, stopping at nothing. Night
after night the story was the same. Instead of enjoying
the good things of home, I went to the places of sin.

It was while living in sin that I joined the army, becoming a member of the Red Arrow Division. On April
18, 1915, disgusted and discouraged, I wandered down
Monroe Avenue and turned down Market Street toward
the City Rescue Mission. A group of people were singing hymns outside of the Mission, and I stopped to lis-

ten. When these people finished singing, Mel Trotter, God bless him, asked the crowd to come into the Mission for services. I went inside and took a back seat—just in case I wanted to leave in a hurry. A man stood up and gave his testimony as to how God had turned him from wickedness. That set me to thinking, "If God could do that for him, there must be hope for me—bad sinner that I am."

When the invitation was given, I started for the front, and that night at 8:15 I cried my heart out to God, and God lifted my burden and saved my soul.

That was forty-one years ago—and I still remember it. Although, like everyone else, I have had my troubles since becoming a Christian, I have had God's blessing upon my life.

In 1917, our outfit went to France, where I was wounded three times. Years later in 1951, I had to go to the veteran's hospital in Chicago. I was there for five years and during that time I went from ward to ward telling the boys about Jesus. Over the period of years, I saw two hundred of these men give their hearts to God.

CHAPTER SEVEN

World War and Spiritual Conflict

WHEN WORLD WAR I BROKE OUT, Mel Trotter offered to work in the camps through the YMCA. "That was a wonderful experience," he said. "More than fifteen thousand men professed conversion. I was in fifty-four different camps in ten months."

A clause in the contract between the Allies and the YMCA called for the Mission workers to amuse as well as minister to the soldiers. So after a prizefight, or a wrestling match, or a movie, Mel would speak, and then another entertainment would follow. Mel arranged to bring in a gospel quartet, the American Four, which would cover the entertainment clause and still give the group the whole evening for their evangelistic work.

"We began in Oglethorpe," said Mel, "then Chattanooga, and went from coast to coast, from the Gulf of Mexico to the Great Lakes, and ended at Camp Merritt when the flu [epidemic of 1918] closed the camp."

Homer Hammontree was with Mel from the beginning. "I had met Mr. Trotter at the funeral of a mutual friend of ours," said Homer. "I sang at the funeral. When the service was over, Mr. Trotter told of the great opportunity he had, with his male quartet, to reach the soldiers with the good news of salvation in sermon and song."

Mel said to Homer, "I wish you were with the quartet and me in this work." In a short time, Homer joined Mel Trotter and the American Four, traveling up and down the land, singing and leading the singing for the boys in khaki. For twenty months, those six men carried the good news of salvation to about a half million soldiers.

"How that man could hold the attention of the boys as he spoke like lightning!" said Homer Hammontree. "The YMCA huts were crowded everywhere we went. One night Mel was preaching, had been going very fast for about ten minutes, when my chair gave way and I measured my length backwards on the stage! The boys roared! Mr. Trotter jerked out his watch and said, 'Wait a minute, fellows. Ham does that every night at just eight o'clock. He is ten minutes late now!'

"Then, turning like lightning, he was in his message again, preaching as only he could preach. We kept no records, but at the close of the war it was estimated that something like sixteen thousand soldiers had come out for the Lord."

Satan hates such preaching. If he cannot succeed in deceiving and luring Christians away to ruin, he will use every means he can devise to prevent them from leading others out of darkness. He tries to spoil the usefulness, hinder the work, and decrease the rewards of Christians who endanger his kingdom. We are never free from him, and Mel Trotter was no exception to the rule.

The armistice marked the end of World War I, but Mel Trotter was about to face a personal conflict. After twenty months in the army mission, he returned home to find everything gone that is dear to the heart of man. His wife had left him.

"It seemed to me it was my first quarrel with God," he said. "Romans 8:28 came to my rescue: 'For we know that all things work together for good to them that love God, to them who are called according to His purpose.'

"The heavens seemed brass when I attempted to pray it through. I wanted Him to tell me why, but there seemed no answer. The Devil told me that I was perfectly justified in ending it all; that God had gone completely back on me. Friends who had been very intimate refused to speak to me on the streets.

"I was taken through court on the most horrible charge, and the trial, which began with taking depositions in January of 1922, closed in September. While I was thoroughly vindicated by the decree, I became a marked man literally around the world."

Many good friends, though, stood by Mel through thick and thin. "Were I to try to name them," said Mel, "I am sure I would neglect mentioning someone who was very dear to me. But I must mention one."

Homer Hammontree never left Mel's side, but "Ham" was compelled to go to Northfield to fill a conference engagement. He wanted to cancel, but Mel forbade him.

"I took him to the train," said Mel, "went back to my room in the big Mission building, and the darkness seemed so great I could almost cut it with a knife. It grew so terrible I threw myself full length on the floor and asked God to take me home."

It is true that "whom the Lord loveth he chasteneth." It is also true that the Lord chastens out of mercy. "He came to me in all the tenderness of a mother, a father, and lover," said Mel Trotter. "How can I tell it. That night I learned of the permissive will of God. God permits things, of which He is not the author. But 'He never allows you to be tempted above that which you are able, but will with every temptation provide a way of escape, that ye may be able to bear it' (1 Cor. 10:13).

"All through that night I learned that if I would reign with Him, I must suffer with Him, for 'the servant is not greater than his Lord.' He revealed to me that through those darkest hours He was the nearest to me.

But He could not show me that until I was absolutely dependent upon Him. When Mr. Hammontree left, Jesus became my all in all. Before that it was 'Jesus and . . .'; and how I did lean on good old Ham.

"I dare not trust myself to tell you what I know about the companionship of Jesus. 'I will never leave thee nor forsake thee,' and that wonderful night, I began practicing His presence."

There is glory in tribulation, and Mel Trotter is testimony that through it all God had given him victory and greatly enlarged usefulness.

Testimony of John Puls

My mother was a godly woman, and she tried to rear her family in the fear of the Lord. As I grew up working at lumbering in the woods and in the sawmills, however, I lived the rough life of the men with whom I worked. I tried everything that this sinful world had to offer until the age of twenty-six. Then I met and eventually married as fine a girl as anyone could hope for. I loved her very much and tried hard to mend my ways, but the day our first baby was born I came home drunk.

Four years later, at the bedside of my dying mother, I heard her plead with her last words for me to meet her in heaven. I promised I would, but for eight more years I went on in the world's ways, trampling on my mother's love and spurning the precious blood of Christ.

One Sunday night, my wife got me into the City Rescue Mission, where a man by the name of Jim Hill spoke to me about salvation. I became angry with him and called him everything a worldling can lay his tongue to. But he remained calm and patient and explained that Jesus was standing before me, asking, "What will you do with Me?" But he went on to say, "Someday you will

stand before Jesus, and then the question will be, What
will He do with you?" I left the place in anger and promised myself never to return.

Praise God for the Jim Hills in the world! He planted
a seed in my heart, and the question kept coming into
my mind, What will He do with me? The Holy Spirit
was at work.

Finally, on May 6, 1919, I dropped on my knees and
cried my heart out to God to forgive me and save me.
Since then, God has been marvelously good. He has
permitted me to rear five children who are all Christians, and they are all bringing up their families to love
the Lord.

CHAPTER EIGHT

Greatly Enlarged Usefulness

BY 1925, GRAND RAPIDS HAD the reputation of being a city without slums. The Mission building was the largest of its kind in the world and seated twenty-one hundred people. And yet, at the annual winter Bible conferences, hundreds were often turned away or diverted to overflow meetings.

As a result of the continuous revival, scores of men and women were called by God into special work. Among those called were the Stapleys. At the close of an evangelistic meeting conducted by Mel Trotter in Muskegon, Michigan, he had a conversation with Mrs. Stapley. As they talked, Mrs. Stapley said, "But, Mr. Trotter, if I get saved, do I have to quit dancing?"

Mel replied, "You can just go ahead and dance your fool head off, if you want to." He hoped his answer would make her think. A little later Trotter hunted up this lady who was letting the dance keep her from accepting Jesus Christ as her Savior. This time he approached her with an attitude of Christian sympathy and interest. "I meant what I told you," said Mel, "but if you are really truly saved and consecrated to His work, you will not want to dance."

Mrs. Stapley, then and there, accepted Christ as her Savior and Lord. "I thought I was having a good time in the world," she said. "There was nothing I loved to do so much as to dance. But worldly pleasures are not to be compared with the heavenly joys and wealth of the sweet peace I now have with my Lord."

Not long after Mrs. Stapley came to Christ, her husband was saved, and later the Stapley's son, Sid, came to the Lord. At first, Sid was very timid in testimony, but the Lord strengthened him until he was soon out on the street corners, shouting the message of salvation to all who would hear.

The Stapleys served on the Mission staff for many years, Mr. Stapley as building manager and Mrs. Stapley as a women's worker.

All those employed at Missions in other cities were converts, personally trained by Mel Trotter, and for many years Trotter raised the money to run these Missions. Later, however, because of his increasing evangelistic work, this was impossible. Most of the Missions, though, became so highly regarded in their own communities that they were able to raise money from regular subscriptions.

To recruit workers from the ranks of converts, it was first necessary to win converts. The City Rescue Mission attracted prospective converts in a number of ways.

The Mission firmly believed in the power of music to attract people's interest. By the 1920s, organs, cornets, bells, and xylophones all were employed for the regular street meetings, which were held during the summer and were especially blessed of the Lord. Two cars were equipped with bells attached to keyboards. Upon these gospel songs were played, and when the crowd gathered, they were given a rousing address, and Mission workers gave their testimony. Hundreds were saved. In John Ball Park there was a natural hillside amphitheater, and there hundreds heard the Word every Sunday afternoon.

So well organized had the Mission work become among the large employers of labor that leading manu-

facturing concerns were anxious that their men hear the
gospel. In 1924, mission workers held 544 shop meetings, reaching 33,715 men and women. About twenty-
five shops were accessible. The volunteer workers
included ministers, businessmen and women, teachers,
and many others. It seemed that God had set His special seal upon the work, and the community seemed to
recognize God's hand at the City Rescue Mission.

The Mission never conducted a single fund drive.
While it is true that many affluent people were friends
of the Mission, it depended for the most part upon volunteer subscriptions and freewill offerings. Once a year,
at the January Bible conference, Trotter appealed for
funds, and the people responded.

On the day of the appeal, the people were given a de-
tailed account of every cent entrusted to the Mission.
According to the Mission treasurer, in 1923, $18,247.56
was raised in pledges—most of it emanating from Grand
Rapids—and $8,847.56 in plate offerings. The annual re-
port for the year closing 1924 showed receipts totaling
$31,270.55, disbursements of $30,900.73, and a balance
on hand of $368.82. In 1925, the Mission buildings and
their equipment were valued roughly at three hundred
thousand dollars. It was obvious that the Mission greatly
enlarged the usefulness of every dollar it received.

The successful work of the City Rescue Mission did
not go unnoticed by others in the field of evangelism.
Thus, Trotter had for years been in demand for Bible
conference work. For twenty-two years, W. R. Moody
regularly invited Mel to the Northfield General Conference. Mel spoke at Bible conferences at Winona Lake,
Indiana; Old Orchard, Maine; Massanetta Springs, Virginia; Ocean Grove, New Jersey; Cedar Lake, Indiana;
Montrose, Pennsylvania; and other places.

In May 1924, in Memphis, Tennessee, Trotter finished
Billy Sunday's meetings, which Sunday had left on

account of illness. In one week, more than a thousand souls were saved.

Trotter prayed much about where to go, and he followed what he believed to be God's will. In September 1924, he was in Allegan, Michigan, thirty miles from Grand Rapids, and practically the entire high-school student body came forward. During October, he was in a tabernacle meeting in Oskaloosa, Iowa, where one-third of the population attended every meeting and hundreds of people were saved. People all over the United States seemed hungry for the gospel of Christ.

Both in his evangelistic work and in the Mission work itself, Trotter's slogan was "Everlastingly at it." He preached much about the power of God—through the shed blood of Jesus—to save and keep from sin. Jesus is the only antidote for sin. He is still the Great Physician, healing human lives wrecked and ruined by Satan.

As a result of Mel Trotter's introducing the touch of Jesus, thousands of Christians from the United States and Canada could testify to the saving and keeping power of Christ. Everywhere Mel Trotter went he met converts who had been saved in the old City Rescue Mission. By the blessing of God, the usefulness of the work begun in Grand Rapids, Michigan, was being enlarged and lived out in the lives of Christians far beyond the confines of the Midwest. Oh, mighty God, how great thou art!

Testimony of Mr. and Mrs. Gerrit Van Bloemendaal

Gerrit Van Bloemendaal had been brought up in the church in his native Netherlands. "My parents were religious, and some of my aunts and uncles were saved," said Gerrit. "But when I came to this country I neglected the house of God. My bad habits included swearing, smoking, and some drinking. But even so, God was working in my heart, sending Holy Spirit conviction."

For Christmas of 1928, Gerrit received a Bible. Another link in the chain of events that led to Gerrit's conversion was Bill Lindeman's invitation to attend the services at the Mel Trotter Mission. Bill and Gerrit worked together at the Gas Company.

Being in a Mission service was a new experience   for the Van Bloemendaals. "In fact," said Mrs. Van Bloemendaal, "I vowed I would never come again." But she did! Mrs. Van Bloemendaal's limited spiritual knowledge had been gained mostly through her mother's Bible reading and some summer Bible school sessions.

Each time the Van Bloemendaals came to the Mission, Casey Jeltema (one of the Mission converts) would urge them forward at the invitation time. The third Sunday night at the Mission, Gerrit did go to the altar at the invitation time, brother Jeltema walking the aisle with him. George Trotter had preached the sermon on the subject of how "they brought them in from the highways and byways" (Luke 14:23).

When brother Van Bloemendaal rose from his knees, having received the Savior, he was happily surprised to see that his wife and stepdaughter had also come forward to receive the Lord as their Savior. What a night!

For many years, they attended the Sunday night services at the Mission, always ready to tell what the Lord had done for them. How they loved to share their joy and knowledge of the Savior.

I'll Not Remember Your Sins

ONE OF MEL TROTTER'S favorite sermon themes was Christ's forgiveness, for Mel was living proof that God would blot out all of our sins. In the late 1930s, during a sermon on Christ's forgiveness, Mel asked the congregation to turn to Isaiah 43:23–25:

> Thou hast not brought me the small cattle of thy burnt offerings; neither hast thou honoured me with thy sacrifices. I have not caused thee to serve with an offering, nor wearied thee with incense.
>
> Thou hast bought me no sweet cane with money, neither hast thou filled me with the fat of thy sacrifices: but thou hast made me to serve with thy sins, thou hast wearied me with thine iniquities.
>
> I, even I, am he that blotteth out thy transgressions for mine own sake, and will not remember thy sins.

"Just to think," said Mel, "there's no prayers, no offerings, no worship, no weariness with sacrifices, and yet He said, 'I'll forgive you. I blot out your transgressions. I do it for mine own sake. I'll not remember your sins.'"

During the sermon that day, Mel offered a good out-

line of how sins are blotted out: "They're blotted out
from God's Book; they're blotted out with God's hand;
they're blotted out for His sake; and my sins are blotted
out from His memory."

Mel continued,

> I'm going to tell you today that God keeps
> books, but not like what I used to think He did
> when I was a boy. I used to think that every good
> thing I did would be put down, and every bad
> thing I did would be put down, and that when I
> got ready to die, every good thing would add up
> and then the bad ones, and then subtract the dif-
> ference. If I did more in the good, I would go to
> heaven. And if I did more evil than good, I would
> perish. Now I know that isn't so, and yet, I tell
> you, God keeps books. God knows you. And God
> knows every thought and intent of the heart.

Mel then told a story about a boy in Chicago. In a
room at the East Chicago Avenue station, the young man
confessed to his sweetheart that he had killed his father
and mother. Dictaphones were hidden in that room. The
boy came back the next Tuesday and pleaded "not
guilty," but they played the Dictaphone tapes and he
heard his own voice convict himself.

Mel concluded the sermon:

> You know, the funny thing about it is, if Edison
> could do this, don't you think God can do it?
> Every word, even every idle word.
>
> Why, you know the funny thing is, God keeps
> records as well as Edison can do it, even the sins
> of your youth, the feelings, the anger, the things
> you know to be wrong. It's like soft cement.
>
> Thirty years ago Homer Hammontree, down

in Marysville [*sic*], Tennessee, marked his name
in that stuff; it's still there. I saw it, because it
was put in soft cement. Now, if God keeps records
set in cement, there's nothing but eternal pun-
ishment ahead for me.

But you see, there's hope. There's hope in this
text: "I, even I, am he that blotteth out thy transgressions for mine own sake, and I will not remember thy sins."

You see, it's a commercial term. I'm in debt,
and He pays my debt.

It's a technical term—like an ink eradicator. He
has blotted them out.

You see, judgment has gone ahead. My, my,
that's a comfort to me. You see, thank God, the
whole thing has been blotted out.

Mel Trotter was known as a powerful speaker, and
when he had attained almost forty years of service to
God, he wanted to pass along an important message to
those who were just beginning to walk in the way of the
Lord.

You dear ones who are coming along the way
of life should know that it is better further on.
These are days of keenest fellowship and friendship, communion and companionship, and I
would not exchange them for all the world. All
the sore spots are healed. Love has taken their
place.

In fact, just a few weeks ago I went to those
whom I felt had wronged me and asked them to
forgive me for my bitterness and to place all the
blame on me. Now I have peace with the world,
as well as with my wonderful Savior.

I am not unmindful, however, that "Now we

see as in a glass darkly," when in a few days it will be "face to face." "Now we know in part; then we shall know even as also we are known." Looking unto Jesus, "the author and finisher of our faith; who for the joy that was set before him endured the cross, despising the shame, and is set down at the right hand of the throne of God" (Hebrews 12:2).

God bless you all.

Testimony of Casey Vander Jagt

I had a fleet of taxi cabs—not doing a regular legitimate business, but catering more to the man who had a thirst and needed a bootlegger. I had a way of getting the bad men and women together, and it was a very remunerative job.

But my family was about to be broken up. My wife had met me in front of the downtown Mission one night and told me so. Soon after, I happened into a revival meeting that was being held in a tent in Burton Heights. That very night, I was converted.

The next day, I went out and sold my taxi cabs—or turned them back for debt— purchased a truck, and went to work hauling coal. It was pretty hard getting along at first, but I was sure that the Lord who had saved me would keep me, and He did.

I constantly told the story from the very beginning, how I had found the Lord, and how the Lord had found me. I have a great big voice, and I told the story everywhere.

I was unable to read or write, but with the help of the Mission, I learned to print catchy mottoes like "Jesus Saves"; "Get Right With God"; "Jesus Is Coming"; and "How Long Since You Wrote Mother?" I placed these on fence boards, stones, bridges and culverts, or wherever I could find a space. Out of that little start came these road signs that were seen throughout Michigan.

Many Christians question the value of this sort of work, but here's just one incident: Two women were driving and saw my big sign with Romans 6:23: "The wages of sin is death, but the gift of God is eternal life through Jesus Christ our Lord." One woman turned to the other and said, "What can I do to be saved?"

They pulled off to the side of the road and reasoned it out like this: "If Jesus Christ was a gift, and a gift from God, the only way to have that gift is to accept it." Right there on the road that woman was wonderfully saved. That would pay for all the signs I ever put up.

Postscript: Casey Vander Jagt went home to be with the Lord in 1971. He was known far and wide for his great witnessing ministry. People from many walks of life came to know the Lord Jesus Christ through the courageous efforts of this great warrior of the Cross.

God's Soldier Goes Home

THE HEADLINE OF THE *Grand Rapids Herald* told the story:

MEL TROTTER, SOLDIER OF GOD
AND MISSION FOUNDER, DIES

The Lord called Mel Trotter home on Wednesday, September 11, 1940. For more than forty years he had been superintendent of the City Rescue Mission. He died at his summer cottage at Macatawa Park.

Trotter's death is believed to have been due to a heart attack. He was seventy years old and had been at his cottage since returning from Kannapolis, N.C., earlier in the year. He had been in a hospital in Kannapolis, recovering from a heart attack that had placed him near death.

At the last annual meeting, the board of the old City Rescue Mission changed the name of that historic institution to the Mel Trotter Rescue Mission in honor of the man who had been its founder and was its moving spirit for forty years.

An editorial in the *Press* revealed why the downtrodden were drawn to Mel Trotter:

> If we understand God's Word correctly, He would be served by helpfulness to others to see the way of righteousness. He would rejoice that

one had turned from the downward path and
sought the light.

He had given his all in order to bring the sinner to repentance and to help the downtrodden.
Mel Trotter could do this perhaps better than
most men. He had known the ways of the trans-
gressor. One day a small voice whispered to him,
and he heard. From that day on, Mel Trotter gave
his life to the service of God and God's children.

How many men and women Mel Trotter
brought to repentance none ever can know. How
many lives he had saved, how many hungry stom-
achs he had appeased, how many bodies he had
clothed, how many souls he had brought to God
is a secret of God's alone.

People from all walks of life came to the funeral to
pay their respects. Dr. Homer Hammontree, Trotter's
longtime friend, led the service, and he told about Mel's
last song:

I was with Mr. Trotter for a long time, out in
the Lord's work, and I have known him to hold
such a service as this, time after time, and he always wanted the service to be victorious rather
than a time of sadness. We rejoice with him, in
that he has finished his course, kept the faith,
and won the goal. It is a great loss for us and for
the Mission. It is a great gain for him, and so we
would rejoice with him.

Those of you who were at the meeting last
Sunday night will remember that after the service we spent the evening with Mr. Trotter. We
found him so much better. That same evening
we sat at the table with him and laughed and
talked together. Then Howard Hermanson and

I went to the piano and began to sing. The first thing I knew, dear Ole' Boss was standing by my side, singing. We sang a trio, as we had done so many times in days gone by . . . "We Will Understand It Better By and By . . . "

Then he said: "Think of it, Ham, throughout eternity our friendship will abide."

William McCarrell, who had met Mel Trotter many years earlier at Moody Bible Institute, told of Mel's last admonition to him:

In those years [at Moody] I never dreamed it would be my privilege to teach for many years in this great and God-blessed work. For eight years I taught the Friday night class in this Mission.

For some years I was away. Last year I returned, and I never shall forget our last little walk, between this corner and the next, as I left to get the train. As we shook hands, near Monroe Avenue, I knew he was trying to say something that he desired me to remember. He said at last, "Carry on for God, Christ, and the salvation of souls."

Dr. Henry Beets had come to Grand Rapids in 1900, the same year as Mel Trotter. Dr. Beets, representing the local Ministers' Association, related a story about a young boy who in 1709 had been trapped upstairs in his home during a fire:

The boy had sense enough not to try to come down the stairs. He went to a window and a living ladder was formed and little Johnny was saved. It was John Wesley, to whom I am referring, the founder of Methodism. And ofttimes later on he said, "I was saved as a brand from the burning."

God, in His mercy, saves some people from the burning, and He also saved as a brand from the burning our beloved Mel Trotter. Those of us who have heard his story, the story of his conversion, never will forget what he was, until our Lord sovereignly, graciously, lovingly plucked him as a brand out of the burning.

These brands oftentimes are used to do great things, so that God may get the glory. He made great use of this man of God, Melvin E. Trotter, a sinner saved by grace and plucked as a brand from the burning.

Mel Trotter made Grand Rapids a place known throughout the church world in our United States. On one occasion, my wife and I went to Winona Lake, Indiana, hunting for a room. It was hard to find a place, but I happened to say that I came from Grand Rapids. I still remember the smile that came upon the face of the landlady. "Well," she said, "well, if you are from Mel Trotter's town, I will make room for you."

Art Blackmore, the barber who tested his wife's faith, was in 1940 working in a Mission in Erie, Pennsylvania. He represented the Mission men and talked of separation and reunion:

I find in my heart today that I am sort of stricken betwixt the two. My better self tells me that this is a great day of victory. But, somehow, there is a pain way down in my heart that just will not have it so.

As I was sitting here thinking and praying, my mind went back to what a dear old father and mother told me about their daughter who was coming home from China, where she had been for many years as a missionary. They told me what a time the daughter had getting away. The Chinese gathered about her when they knew she was going to leave them. They stayed all night. They prayed and wept and said, "What will we do? We don't know what to do if you go away."

As I sat here today, I have come to see another picture. One was a parting, and the other a home-coming, and what a difference! Precious in the sight of the Lord is the homecoming of His children.

This is a hard day for us, but there is another group of Mission folk over there in glory having a glorious time today. Dear old Herb Sillaway is there; Harry Monroe, Ed Card, whom we used to hear sing from this platform. While we are here and our hearts are very heavy, I am sure there is rejoicing over there.

Then Art described a side of Mel of which not everyone was aware:

We Mission boys loved Mel because he was God's instrument in bringing us to Christ, [but] very few people knew the real Mel Trotter.

I have seen him pray with a poor helpless drunkard, then stand him on his feet and say, "Now go home and get the wife and kiddies and come down to the Mission tonight." Then as they parted, he would slip a dollar bill or a silver dollar in the poor drunkard's hand. I heard one of those men say, as he stood outside the Mission door, after such a parting, "I will die before I spend this dollar for booze." One of those very fellows now is an honored evangelist.

Mel was big in every sense of the word, but he was never too big to be humble in his living. The

other day, when we received the telegram that
Mel had gone, a young man past thirty years of
age stood before me and said, "Do you know why
I loved Mel Trotter?"

Then he told me this story: One time at the
Mission, some of the boys were cutting up,
and there was a little fellow among them, only
ten years old. Mr. Trotter had scolded the boys
and told them to behave, and then he turned
to the little fellow and gave him a reprimand,
too. The little fellow cried and went away. That
night this auditorium was packed with people,
but Mel found the boy and hugged him. Mr.
Trotter said to the boy, "I wronged you this afternoon. I saw your tears and knew how badly
you felt and when I found you weren't one of
the boys who was cutting up, I felt badly, and I
want you to forgive me."

As this young man told me this story the other
day, tears ran down his cheeks, and he said to
me, "Dad, that was one of the greatest incidents
in my life. That is the reason Mel was great. The
Spirit of God was in his life." [The little boy was
Carl Blackmore, the musician and composer.]

When Dr. Lowry, the great songwriter, was
passing away, Fannie Crosby went to see him. She
took his hand and said to him, "Good night,
Doctor, until we meet in the morning." So that
is all I can say to my old pal . . . "Good night,
dear Boss, till we meet in the morning."

Homer Hammontree added a few words that brought
a chuckle to the assemblage:

I used to say to Mel, "Boss, your middle name
ought to be *apologize.*" Mr. Trotter wasn't perfect.

Sometimes he would say the wrong thing. I loved
him because he always would go back and hunt
up the person he had wronged and ask forgiveness. I don't believe he ever got angry at me. We
were together nineteen years, and we never quar-
reled. He used to say it was because of his good
disposition, but I always told him it was on account of mine.

Walter Clark, treasurer of the Mission, represented the
board. Walter knew yet another side of Mel Trotter:

Mel lived a full three-score years and ten—and
eight years more than half of his life he spent in
this peculiar work. It would be a wonderful thing
if we could know even approximately how many
people he has brought into the kingdom.

But the board contacted a side of Mel Trotter
that was a bit different from that of conducting
his regular services. It was more business about
it, and a chance to get a different view of the man,
and the things he did. There was no skull-duggery
about any business with which he had to do. Mel
was a straight-shooter, and everything had to be
done just like that.

Mr. Trotter possessed a keen business sense,
very much so. His outlook was always progres-
sive and generally correct, as evidenced by the
fact that he started in a little old store building
down there on Canal Street, and then a little later
in the building on Market Street, and then on
down to this great building here in which services
have been held for so many years.

One of the biggest men in this town said to
me the other day, "You know, if Mel had elected
to go into business—normal business—instead of

taking up Mission work, he could have put anything over that he might have undertaken."

Why? Because of his great personality and his
ability and his all aroundedness—I don't know
what else to call it——in doing things in a business way. And we are proud of the glorious work
Mel has done.

Homer Hammontree returned to the rostrum:

> Mel Trotter didn't have many outside interests,
> but he loved to go to his Rotary Club every Thurs-
> day noon—he had to be mighty sick if he missed
> that. He often talked about how fine the Rotarians
> were when it came to helping him out. He said,
> "All I have to do is write them, and the goods all
> come pouring into the Mission at Thanksgiving
> and Christmastime."

Dr. John Dykstra, a local pastor, represented the Ro-
tary Club of Grand Rapids. Dr. John expressed what was
surely on many minds that day:

> For twenty-two years, Mel Trotter was a mem-
> ber of the Rotary organization, devoted to the
> ideal of service and its application to personal,
> business, community, and international life. Our
> tribute cannot be better expressed than in these
> words spoken of our friend's Savior and Lord:
> "He went about doing good, for God was with
> him" (Acts 8: 28). Mel exemplified in his life the
> motto of Rotary, "Service Above Self." If every-
> one today to whom he did a good deed were to
> cast a bloom on his casket, he would sleep be-
> neath a wilderness of flowers.
> Surely it is his deep desire that when you and

I come to the end of the road and face the King of Kings and Lord of Lords, that each of us may hear the same words that surely came to Mel Trotter, "Well done, good and faithful servant, enter thou into the joy of thy Lord."

Next to step to the rostrum was Dr. Ironside, who had been with Mel Trotter on a visit to the British Isles. In a stirring eulogy, Dr. Ironside presented an invitation Mel Trotter would have heartily applauded:

Mr. Trotter had said he didn't want any long sermons at his funeral, just happy testimonies of those who were saved by grace and knew what it meant to live for God. One Scripture came home to me while I was listening to these messages: "There is joy in the presence of the angels of God over one sinner that repenteth."

Mel Trotter knew Christ. When he was a poor, lost sinner, he was introduced to Christ. He could say: "Jesus sought me when a stranger, Wandering from the fold of God, He to rescue me from danger, Interposed His precious blood."

Mel was lost, and he wasn't ashamed to tell people just that. I think one is safe in saying that no one of us would be more ready and willing to correct the mistakes we make in life than he.

If he were able to speak to us today, he would have the same message as he had throughout the years. I can almost hear him say, "Don't take up all the time talking about me. There may be some unsaved people in this great auditorium. There may be some people here who don't know Christ today. Oh, don't, don't lose the opportunity. Tell them that there is no other name under heaven given among men whereby we must be saved. Tell

them that Christ died for the ungodly, the un-
worthy; tell them that the Son of Man has come
to seek and to save that which was lost. Don't lose
the opportunity to tell them."

Oh what a wonderful thing it would be if, at
this service, precious souls would come to Jesus,
and find the Savior who meant so much to our
dear brother.

Homer Hammontree closed the service with one additional thought:

I want to give myself anew to the Lord Jesus
Christ, that I may carry on the work that the Lord
has called me to do, and I believe I speak for every
Christian here. With that determination, may we
go out of this service to dedicate our lives anew
to the Lord's service.

Thus ended the earthly life of God's faithful servant.
We know that there was joy in heaven as Mel Trotter
entered the gate, but the work he started continued after
him. What to some might seem like the end, is only the
beginning!

Testimony of Lou Shy,
Galewood Mission Superintendent

My favorite verse is 2 Corinthians 5:17: "If any man be
in Christ, he is a new creature: old things are passed
away; behold, all things are become new."

I was brought up in a country Methodist Sunday
school, but I never accepted Jesus Christ as my Savior.
At the age of fourteen, I drifted away into the world,
declaring that I could get by without the Lord and the

church.

But sin is no respecter of persons. I drifted deeper and deeper into it. I thought I was having a good time, but God says, "Be sure your sin will find you out" (Num. 32:23). At the age of twenty-eight, I was a cigarette fiend and a drunkard. I am ashamed of my past life, but I am not ashamed of Jesus Christ and His saving grace.

One night in 1923, I walked into the old City Rescue Mission. I heard many testimonies of former down-and-outers and up-and-outers, and they all said they were saved by grace. I said in my heart, "This must be what I need."

When the invitation was given, I raised my hand during prayer, and later when invited, I went forward and that night Jesus saved me. Now I can say, the Lord not only saves, but He keeps and satisfies. Salvation is a gift anyone may have by accepting Christ as his or her personal Savior. "I am not ashamed of the gospel of Christ: for it is the power of God unto salvation to every one that believeth" (Rom. 1:16).

CHAPTER ELEVEN

The Work Goes On

WHAT HAPPENS TO A MINISTRY when the dynamic founder and leader leaves the scene? For forty years the Mission was under the direction of Mel Trotter. But through the years Mel had trained many young men for leadership positions.

Both John Shy and Mel Johnson served the Lord well in the first years after Mel Trotter's death— John as interim superintendent, Mel in charge of the radio ministry, music, and young people's work.

John Shy was brought up in a fine home where the seven children—three boys and four girls—were loved by their parents. John attended Sunday school and church regularly, and his ambition was to become a building contractor when he finished school.

John's sister invited him to attend a Bible conference held at the City Rescue Mission in Grand Rapids. John accepted, not necessarily interested in the Bible teaching but in the fine music. "What a thrill," said John, "to hear that vast audience sing the good old gospel songs!"

The Conference was held in January, the week of the nineteenth, which was Mel Trotter's spiritual birthday. And each year Mel gave his testimony of how God had transformed his life.

"I had heard Mr. Trotter preach some years before," said John. "It made a great impression on my life. When

I attended the Bible conference with my sister, I was convicted of my need of a Savior. Although I had never gone into the depths of sin, I was just as much in need of a Savior as Mel Trotter was the night he entered the Pacific Garden Mission in Chicago. On January 19, 1925, as a twenty-year-old furniture worker, I met the Lord."

John had a burning desire to work for the Lord, and so while employed in a factory during the day, he was down at the Mission five or six nights a week, witnessing and endeavoring to win souls to Christ. On weekends, he took part in the young people's work, jail work, and Sunday school as a volunteer worker.

One night, Mr. Trotter called John into his office after the evening service.

"Where do you work?" Mel asked. "What are your future plans for your life?"

John answered, "I would like to go into mission work full time."

"We've been watching you for the past year," said Mel. "We've been praying that the Lord would prepare you for mission work. There's an opening here at the Mission. Would you be interested?"

Workers at the Mission had to be willing to do everything in the field of rescue—janitor work, preaching, witnessing, jail work, open-air work, shop work, financing, pulpit supply, and many other tasks, including teaching Sunday school.

Mel Johnson had been a student in John Shy's Sunday school class, but his family had a history with the old City Rescue Mission. Mel Johnson's grandfather, known as drunken Hank Johnson, was miraculously saved at the Rescue Mission, and Mel's dad, Stanley Johnson, was given a new life late one night after hearing a railroad evangelist present the gospel at the Mission.

"Dad came home and knelt beside the old furnace in our house," said Mel, "and gave his heart to Christ. He

then called me and wanted me to be the first to know
about it, since he knew I had accepted Christ as my
Savior a few months earlier."

Mel became a part of the Rescue Mission program,
and Mel Trotter sent him to the Moody Bible Institute
in Chicago. After his graduation, Trotter hired Mel
Johnson to be his director of music, radio, and young
people.

Mel Johnson's experiences at the Mel Trotter Mission
reflect those of every worker who served the Lord there.
"We learned life's most valuable lessons at the Mission,"
said Mel, and he listed those lessons. "We learned to
work long and diligently." Mel was pledged to work in
whatever capacity he was called—in the clothes room,
taking a speaker to his hotel room, or sitting down across
from a hungry man at a restaurant.

"We learned to take orders." Mel never argued or said
that it was not in his job description. "I don't recall ever
getting one. Mel Trotter gave us opportunities to be
creative and to implement many of our ideas.

"We learned to be on time." One of Mel's responsi-
bilities was a thirty-minute morning program on the
city's largest commercial station. He learned to get up
early and be at the studio every morning at six-thirty.

"We learned the art of patience." Mel didn't watch
the clock during long meetings. "I didn't care how long
they lasted. I was with my friends, and my friends felt
like I did.

"We learned how to witness." While at Moody Bible
Institute, Mel took his assignments in witnessing seriously. He had learned how to witness from Mel Trotter
before entering as a freshman at Moody.

"We learned to do things we didn't like to do—ugly
things." Mel learned what it was to kneel beside a smelly
drunk . . . "and then walk him home so he wouldn't stop
by the bar or beat up his family when he arrived home.

"We learned to see the needs of others." In the winter people came in without coats and necessary footwear. The needs were serious ones, and Mel learned that people trusted the Mission and relied on its help.

"We learned that God supplies every need." Mel watched in amazement while department stores called for mission trucks and donated racks of clothes. He marveled at the way businessmen supplied food for the hungry.

"We learned to pray in faith and to expect answers. One of the greatest heritages in my life at the Mission was to watch God work and see great results.

"We learned to be excited about what we were doing." Mel became a part of his coworkers' activities, and he rejoiced in the Lord's blessing on their work.

"We learned to study and to preach." Some nights with only seven or eight in a meeting, Mel learned to give as much of his energy and heart to that small group as he would to a Sunday meeting of twenty-five hundred people.

"We learned to be prepared and let the Spirit of God use His Word. That was the only effective way to meet the spiritual needs of people."

Most important, Mel saw results and learned that, no matter who led the work, the work had to go on. He learned to believe and accept that the Mission had to be "everlastingly at it."

Shortly after he went on staff in August 1940, Mel organized a Saturday morning club for boys aged nine to fourteen. The club became a singing group, consisting of about a hundred voices. When they gave a concert at the Mission, they sang to a full house of more than two thousand people. Wearing white shirts and black ties, the group became known as the White Shirt Brigade.

Mel also formed softball teams in the summertime, and they played basketball in the winter months.

During the days of transition after Trotter's death, Mel thought that this program, in part, kept the Mission going. Because of the outreach to the boys, many of the parents were also brought in.

At the age of fourteen, the boys graduated into a group called the King's Ambassadors, which sang at the annual International Gideon Convention held in Grand Rapids in 1941. Mel attributed the success of the program to the constancy and consistency of being with the boys, and everyone was welcome because the Mission was nondenominational.

One of the boys became a professional basketball player for the Los Angeles Lakers, another became a neurosurgeon, and still another became a psychologist. Many of them went into full-time Christian work as preachers or missionaries.

Mel was also one of the founders of the Children's Bible House, originating in Grand Rapids. The Boys' Clubs became the first audience of the *Children's Bible Hour*, a live radio program at the time.

A microphone was placed in front of one young lad. When asked his name, he said, "Charlie" (Charles VanderMeer), who later became "Uncle Charlie," the director of the *Children's Bible Hour* for many years.

It all began at the Mission. The work Mel Trotter began in 1900 would go on because men and women had dedicated themselves to continuing God's work. Who can fathom what the Lord can do with those who are sold out completely to Him?

Mel Johnson Remembers

I remember the "Say-So Time." Mel Trotter always waited for the young people in attendance to get up and "say so." As a freshman in high school, I gave my first testimony on a Saturday night. I was seated between my grandpa and my uncle, who were both converted at the Mission, and who were strong stalwarts of the faith. Everybody had testified one Saturday night except me, and Mel Trotter waited for me.

Finally he said, "There's a young man out there that I know wants to say something," and in coordination with that speech, my grandpa and my uncle lifted me to my feet, and I found myself standing. I said, "I'm glad Jesus saved me. Amen." After I had sat down, the great Mel Trotter said, "That's the finest testimony I have ever heard!" He made it easy for me to stand up and "say so."

ʊ CHAPTER TWELVE

Bearing the Torch

THE OLD GOSPEL SONG SAYS, "The Light of the world is Jesus." But in the 1940s it was a dark world. The thunder of war rumbled from across the seas—Hitler, Mussolini, the Nazis, the fascists, the communists, Japan, and the bombing of Pearl Harbor. After December 7, 1941, America was involved full-scale in World War II, and young men left to defend our shores.

In spite of gas and sugar rationing, shortages of coffee, and the need for coupon books, the hungry still needed to be fed and the naked clothed, and the gospel continued to be proclaimed through the Mel Trotter Mission.

The Mission endeavored to maintain its normal functions, and the January annual Bible conference was held in 1942. Homer Hammontree directed, and Dr. Harry Rimmer came from Fort Dix, New Jersey, where he had recently established a large gospel center, ministering to thousands of soldiers.

The Mission, too, did its part in the war effort. One of the slogans during those days was, "A slip of the lip could sink a ship." Thus, an announcement was made in connection with the radio ministry: "I trust that everyone understands that requests are not being honored on broadcasts during this time because of orders from the war department."

Mrs. Stapley and the women's auxiliary worked on an order for five thousand pairs of slippers for men of the armed services who had been wounded or hospitalized. The names of eighteen hundred servicemen were on the prayer list at the Mission, and each had been contacted by the Mission staff.

The army took over the Pantlind Hotel (now the Amway Grand Plaza) to house the weather school, which brought many servicemen into the city. As an outreach ministry, the Mission maintained a center for servicemen that gave them a place to relax and enjoy free refreshments.

In January 1944, World War II still raged. The Mission continued to shine a light, both in the community through its local ministries and into the long night of conflict through its war ministries. For the annual Bible conference that year, George Weir—the famous coronetist from Canada—and Dr. Homer Rodeheaver, singer and trombonist who for twenty years traveled with Billy Sunday—took part in the music program.

Also in 1944, the Mission acquired a new superintendent, Rev. Fred C. Zarfas, who replaced John Shy. John later went to Muskegon, Michigan, to help set up a gospel program in that Mission. A short time later, he entered Grace Theological Seminary at Winona Lake, Indiana, and then founded the Flint City Mission in 1950. He directed the work there for thirty years.

By 1945 peace had returned to the world, and another change was announced in the *Mission Messenger,* the newsletter for the Mel Trotter Mission: "Glenn Calhoun has been called to the Mel Trotter Mission as youth leader and music director. Calhoun is a graduate of the Pastor's Course at Moody Bible Institute. From there he went to Wheaton College. He has served as assistant in a church in Cheyenne, Wyoming, and before coming to Grand Rapids, pastored a church in Waterloo, Nebraska."

Mel Johnson, whom Glenn replaced, left the Mission

to work with Youth for Christ as the Chicago director, and then as the vice president. During his years of service for the Lord, Mel worked on forty-eight books and pamphlets as author or as compiler. As a member of the Northwestern College (Minnesota) board of trustees for many years, Mel acted as chairman for eighteen years. He was the 1967 Moody Alumnus of the Year and became an honorary alumnus of both Northwestern and Cornerstone Colleges. He went on to receive the Honorary Doctor of Humane Letters from Cornerstone College (now Cornerstone University) in Grand Rapids, Michigan, on May 16, 1997. The doctorate is awarded to individuals who have exhibited exemplary professionalism, communication, scholarship, and Christian character in their lives.

For the 1947 Bible conference, Rev. Fred C. Zarfas extended the following invitation:

> Dear Friends: We welcome you to the forty-eighth annual Meeting and Bible conference. We meet amid the distress of nations, with unrest, starvation, and suffering the lot of millions. The threat of a third world war is ever upon us. The problems in our own beloved United States are legion. Never before was the need for such a Bible conference as necessary as it is now. Believing the Bible to be the living and powerful Word of God, we invite you to attend this important conference.

The Mission board and staff had, over the preceding years, seen much accomplished. The main Mission building underwent remodeling, and, once the dust settled, the sidewalk needed paving. The Branch Mission got a new roof and a nicely painted front. And once the old cornice was torn off, the building had a more modern appearance. There was much left to do at the Branch, however.

Carpentry projects and new plumbing would be needed to bring the building up to standards for the men's residence. Once the work got under way, however, there would be bills and more bills.

Some of the regular expenses from the previous year called for less than had been budgeted, but with continually rising prices, many of the costs would be higher. It was expected that the needs of the Mission for 1948 would be approximately $42,500, and for 1949 the treasurer reported that the Old Lighthouse would need approximately $40,000 for operating expenses.

But Mel Trotter used to say, "You can't beat God in giving," and that had been proven over and over. As Superintendent Zarfas said, "God takes care of those who take care of His work."

The last Bible conference of the 1940s marked the close of a tumultuous decade, one that witnessed world war as well as the start of economic recovery, and that changed the way we looked at the world. It seemed fitting that the music for the Bible conference that closed such a momentous decade was placed in the charge of Rev. and Mrs. Elbert Tindley of Lansing, Michigan, internationally known African American gospel singers.

The Mission's board and staff looked back with gratitude at what God had accomplished over almost five decades, and they looked with anticipation to the Mel Trotter Rescue Mission's golden anniversary—fifty years of shining a light through the Word of God, helping those who were unable to help themselves.

Testimony of Rev. and Mrs. Henry Boersma

Our wonderful Savior found us in a life of religion, but it was through the ministry of Dr. William McCarrell that we learned about our need of a Savior. We were both brought up in homes where we were taught to go to Sunday school and church.

After we were married, we attended a class for many weeks of instruction before joining the church. We gave answers to the questions and were received into the church, but we were told nothing about the new birth.

Like most people, we had a deep interest in the future, so when Dr. McCarrell came to the Mel Trotter Mission with a series of studies on the book of Revelation, we received great blessings from it. But we were still unsaved.

The following winter Dr. McCarrell again came to the Mission for a series of studies on the book of Romans. During the study of the third chapter, we were both convicted of our need of a Savior. In our own home we received Him into our hearts and were born again by the Spirit of God.

A number of years later, we served as home missionaries and engaged in visitation evangelism for Calvary Undenominational Church of Grand Rapids.

There is no end to what the Lord can do with the life of one soul totally committed to Him. It is like the ripple effect of a small pebble tossed into a pond—it never ends.

CHAPTER THIRTEEN

The Golden Jubilee

TIMES CHANGE. PEOPLE CHANGE. Places change. But what a comfort to know that we serve a God who never changes, and that Jesus Christ is "the same yesterday, today, and forever."

The year 1950 marked the golden anniversary of Rescue Mission work in Grand Rapids—fifty years serving from the Old Lighthouse. A special fiftieth anniversary service was held on Thursday, February 2, at the Park Congregational Church in downtown Grand Rapids. The first organizational committee of the old City Rescue Mission had met there fifty years earlier, and it was fitting that the golden anniversary celebration be held there.

The Park Church choir presented a special music program for the anniversary, and the American Four Quartet, the original male quartet that had traveled with Mel Trotter during World War I, thrilled the audience with a reunion performance.

Although the year of the golden anniversary was marked by thanksgiving and celebration, 1950 and 1951 were marked also by the challenge of changes in leadership at the Mission. Rev. Fred Zarfas resigned and left the work at the Mission, and Bob Ingersoll agreed to fill in for a few months as acting superintendent.

Bob had a long history with the Mission, beginning

with the old City Rescue Mission. "When it seemed no
one cared," he said, "when the courts gave up, and loved
ones said they had done all they could, it was the darkest day of my life."

Bob was in the Grand Rapids jail when Mel Trotter
came to see him. "Sin had wrecked my life," said Bob.
"I had no home, no friends, no hope within or without. Mr. Trotter told me the story of Jesus and His love,
and I became a new creature."

By 1950, Ingersoll had became director of the International Evangelistic Association of Winona Lake, Indiana, but interrupted his work to act as interim director
until a permanent director could be appointed. But it
soon became necessary for Bob to leave Grand Rapids
to take up where he had left off in the evangelistic field.

Once again, the Mission was without a leader. In January 1951, Rev. John W. Kershaw of Bridgeport, Connecti-
cut, arrived to serve as interim superintendent. His
ministry met with a very good response. There was a
definite improvement in the relations between the Mission and the evangelical churches in the city. He worked
out a monthly schedule whereby a number of churches
and other Christian organizations were responsible for
meetings in the main Mission, a contribution that proved
most helpful during the time when no permanent superintendent was in charge.

In looking over the schedule of preachers for that
period, the name of a local preacher is prominent because he occupied the Mission pulpit in the Sunday night
services no less than fourteen times. Time and again it
was evident that Rev. George Bontekoe was indeed the
Lord's messenger for the need of the hour.

When it became necessary for Rev. Kershaw to leave,
the choice of an interim superintendent was quickly
made. To the people of Grand Rapids and the outlying
communities, the name of Peter Quist was already fa-

miliar because of his activities as director of Youth for Christ for this city and as the announcer for the *Morning Mission*. Peter was another example of God's gracious provision for the needs of the Mel Trotter Mission. Peter's title, though, was interim superintendent, and soon it was time for Peter to go back for his final year at the Grand Rapids School of the Bible and Music in preparation for the ministry.

The Mission was still without a permanent superintendent. Then the September 1951 issue of the *Mission Messenger* gave this exciting witness to God's faithfulness:

> At this time, as we look forward in glad anticipation to the arrival of Rev. and Mrs. Claude J. Moore, we pause to take a backward look over the past year, a period when the Old Lighthouse has been without a permanent superintendent.
>
> How good God has been in watching over His work and in keeping the Mel Trotter Mission everlastingly at it. The work has gone on—in some ways has increased in volume, effect, and approval. The needy are still receiving help and encouragement when all other sources have failed them. The lost, the backslidden, and the perplexed continue to find the answer to their problems in the all-sufficient One, the Lord Jesus Christ.
>
> Much of the success of the past year is to be attributed to the friends of the Mission, loyal supporters who have given of their means and time to carry on the program, and to those who have stepped into the breach to keep the gospel lights all trimmed and burning.

Claude and Grace Moore were to arrive September 12, 1951. Claude began his ministerial training in 1922

and was ordained at Bowmanville Congregational
Church in Chicago. He had just retired as president of
the International Union of Gospel Missions and was still
on the executive board. He had been in Rescue Mission
work since 1936, having served as assistant superintendent at the Pacific Garden Mission, and for the past eight
years as superintendent of the Union Gospel Mission
of Jamestown, New York.

Grace Moore served as co-superintendent of the Mission with her husband and was in charge of the women's
work there. She had received her Bible training at
Moody Bible Institute of Chicago. Grace had always
wanted to go to Africa as a missionary. Her health, however, prohibited her from getting to the mission field.
Thus, she followed a nursing profession before entering Christian work.

The Moores came to Grand Rapids with many years
of experience in mission work, and they were what the
Mel Trotter Mission needed at that time in its history.
They served as a bridge, linking current ministries of
the Mission to the work that lay ahead.

When the Moores arrived in Grand Rapids, they
found the Mission work to be vigorous and effective,
but their first five weeks with the Mission were slow
because of the Key to Life Group, citywide evangelistic
meetings led by Jack Shuler. Most of the Mission meetings during these first weeks had a low turnout, but the
prayer meetings were doing well.

Also, by 1951, the radio ministry enjoyed widespread
coverage, sending the gospel message in word and song.
Morning Mission had been a continuous blessing to the
community for more than sixteen years. The Sunday
school programs, too, were robust, with classes for all
ages.

The jail ministry had been helping a large number of
men and women get started on new lives. The Branch

Mission was an ideal setup for the rehabilitation phase of the work.

The home visitation ministry continued to be active in both homes and hospitals. Local bakeries donated some five hundred loaves of bread, dozens of doughnuts, cookies, and other baked goods each week for the Mission to deliver to homes. Also the Mission has been able to provide almost all of the clothing needed by the families that were visited.

But the Moores saw areas in the ministry that would require change to meet the needs ahead. The Branch Mission had not been able to function as the board and all others would have liked. With the addition of Pat Walmsley to the staff as co-manager with Brother "Mac" McDonald, the Branch soon began to serve hundreds of meals and provide lodgings for scores of transients and local men. A number of those men confessed our Lord as Savior, and some of them were growing nicely in the grace of God.

The Mission welcomed a new music director in Eddy Davis. This preacher's son served Satan and sin for many years before yielding to his father's God in the Cleveland City Mission. From that moment, Eddy dedicated his life to the service of the Christ, who had saved him.

Grace Moore started a new Saturday morning children's Bible class. The Moores loved children, and the class provided an opportunity to reach children who were unchurched. A good motto to follow in working with children is, "Win the boys and girls for Christ before they learn how to resist the Holy Spirit."

Every Saturday morning, children from neighborhoods surrounding the Mission came in for a children's meeting. The average attendance ran about 125, with the children ranging in age from five to fourteen. Grace Moore was an animated Bible storyteller, and a room packed with restless kids didn't phase her one bit. If they became noisy, she just lowered her voice. The rowdy ones suddenly quieted down and sat on the edge of their seats to catch every word she said.

The children learned songs, and their voices could make the walls shake. As they learned the words to songs, memorized Bible verses, and heard about Jesus and His love, many children came through those days changed. They took Jesus into their hearts and lives, and each week there were those who made a decision to follow Jesus.

Claude Moore had at one time been a chef, and the children's meeting program included a warm meal. Claude said, "This is probably the only warm meal most of these children get all week. Mostly they survive on peanut butter and jelly sandwiches."

While the children were taught the Word of God, they also had a crash course in social behavior. The smaller children lined up first for lunch, and then the older ones stood in line behind them. They marched downstairs to eat, singing "Onward Christian Soldiers." The tables were set with napkins and silverware, and no one sat down until after Mr. Moore prayed. Then the boys had to make sure the girls were seated first. A meal was served, usually macaroni and cheese or spaghetti and meatballs, along with milk, rolls, and other nutritious goodies.

When the children ate, it was obvious that they were hungry, and there was plenty of food for seconds. The only requirement was that the children raise their hands when they wanted more.

But the Moores' concern for the children did not stop at their physical and material needs. Grace and Claude were especially concerned with meeting the children's spiritual needs. Saving souls is, after all, the ultimate purpose of a rescue mission.

Claude Moore took seriously the responsibility of lost

Mel Trotter (1870–1940)

Trotter Tabernacle

501. City Rescue Mission, Grand Rapids, Mich.

The former Smith Opera House was bought by the City Rescue Mission and formally opened for service on September 20, 1907.

Sunday school children outside the Mel Trotter Mission

Mel Trotter and Homer Hammontree

George Bontekoe at WFUR Radio Station

Mel Trotter

The interior of the Monroe Avenue location following the move from the Market Street site

The historic pulpit first used by Mel Trotter

A view of the crowd attending one of the annual Bible conference sessions

The 1912 Mission picnic at Jenison Park

Mel Trotter and a display of Thanksgiving baskets ready for distribution to the city's needy

The American Four, a gospel quartet led by Mel Trotter (front right), traveled from camp to camp during World War I, entertaining the troops and bringing the message of salvation.

Mrs. Sophie Boughner (1876–1951) was one of the Mission's first converts and she faithfully served there for almost fifty years.

The former Smith Opera House on Market Street was the home of the City Rescue Mission for fifty years.

Children were brought in by bus to Sunday school.

The bar from the old Smith Opera House was used by the Mission as the reception counter.

Maranatha men enjoying the meal at their regular Thursday noon meeting

Mel Trotter

The Women's Auxiliary busy at Mission sewing machines

Sidney Stapley, the Mission's printer

George Bontekoe

Mel Trotter

souls. Toward the end of the 1951 annual report, he added a postscript to the list of facts and figures, and he shared his heart: "We know better than anyone living our inability and insufficiency to carry the load of such a work as this. Our only hope is that our Lord will carry the load for us."

At the Mel Trotter Mission, it appeared that the Lord had not only carried the load but also had done it economically. "There is no place in all the world," said Moore, "where a dollar does more for the cause of Christ than in a rescue mission."

The year-end treasurer's report supported Moore's sentiments about the cost-effectiveness of rescue mission work. In spite of supporting the ongoing ministries and adding new ones, the Mel Trotter Mission finished the year in the black: cash on hand as of December 31, 1951, was $740.

The year 1952 began as it had ever since 1900 with the annual Bible conference in January. Dr. S. Franklin Logsdon, pastor of the Moody Memorial Church in Chicago, visited the Mel Trotter Mission for the first time during the conference. He had heard much about the work in Grand Rapids but was amazed to see it in person. After the close of the conference, he sent a letter that was almost lyrical in its description of the Mission:

> Reports are never so illuminating as actual experience. As I surveyed the environs of the erstwhile arena of worldliness, it was a veritable benediction to my own soul to realize that, for these many years, the old theatre has echoed to the dear Old Story that never grows old. Now preachers stand where performers stood. Now it is the proclamation of the Word, where once it was the pleasure of the world. Now it is a place of lusty hallelujahs instead of lustful hilarity.

The energy described in Dr. Logsdon's letter seemed to set the pace for the Mel Trotter Mission for the rest of the year. In March 1952, there was an aura of excitement. The March newsletter announced the coming of Winifred J. Larson. Winifred was widely recognized throughout the gospel music world as the "Kate Smith of Gospel Singers," and she was visiting the Mel Trotter Mission on March 15 and 16. She would be with Youth for Christ Saturday evening and then at the Sunday evening service.

On the heels of Winifred Larson's visit came an announcement in the April newsletter heralding the revival of the old Friday night Bible class. Many workers who had been with the Mission since the days of the old City Rescue Mission remembered those inspiring and uplifting Friday nights. Dr. Philip Newell—son of the well-known Bible teacher, preacher, and writer, Dr. William R. Newell—would be teaching the class. Philip was the dean of student affairs at Moody Bible Institute, and he held a Bible class in Milwaukee every Tuesday evening, which had become a great blessing to that city and community. It was hoped that reviving the Friday night classes would bring a similar blessing to the Mel Trotter Mission and to the city of Grand Rapids.

In May, Dr. Homer Rodeheaver came to the Mission. Dr. Rodeheaver had for many years been with Billy Sunday, making one of the greatest teams that ever preached and sang the gospel.

Also in that eventful year of 1952, the open-air meetings were reinstated. The old truck that had been used for so many years to the glory of the Lord was put back into running order that summer. Preceding the regular service at the Branch Mission, street meetings were held, and there was opportunity to pray with men as a result of almost every street meeting.

The year 1952 provided an uplift for the ministries

and its workers and a facelift for the main Mission building. Members of the Converts Club, a group that originated at the branch Mission, painted the offices and chapel. The Converts Club thrilled the hearts of the Mission staff as they watched the group working and growing together in the grace of the Lord. When in the Converts' Bible classes, the members sat at attention, eager to learn God's Word, and when they bowed their heads, murmuring together in prayer meetings, their simple faith and pure hearts were evident. When possible, members of the club visited the services at the main Mission, where they were afforded the fellowship of folks from different walks of life.

The decade of the fifties began with the golden anniversary of the Mel Trotter Mission. It welcomed a new superintendent and hosted well-known figures in the field of evangelism. But the decade was not over yet. There would be more efforts to reach the lost, more souls drawn into the fold, and more new hands to do the work of God from the Old Lighthouse.

Mildred (Zeilstra) Koning Remembers

A popular song in 1921, the year I was born, was "I Found a Million Dollar Baby in the Five and Ten Cent Store." My father used to sing it to me, telling me that I was his million dollar baby.

When I was seven years old, my parents divorced, and my father left me, an only child, in the care of my mother. I never wanted to hear that "Million Dollar Baby" song again.

But God had a plan for our lives. He led Mom and me to the City Rescue Mission. It was in an old, beautiful former opera house at the corner of Market and Louis Streets in downtown Grand Rapids. It was here I

found a Friend who would never leave me. He gave me
a new song: "When you know Him, when you know Him,
you'll love Him just as others do. A happy morn will
dawn for you, when you know my Jesus, too."

Mel Trotter told me to call him Pops, and I knew I
had a papa who had introduced me to the heavenly
Father. Pops took me into his home like a daughter and
baptized me in Lake Michigan when I was twelve years
old. On my sixteenth birthday, he gave me my Bible.

In September 1940, Pops was supposed to walk me
down the aisle and present me to my husband, Seymour
Koning. But once again, God had other plans. He called
Pops to heaven the night before the wedding. But I did
not walk down the aisle alone. I was on the arm of Jesus.
And He's been holding me ever since.

CHAPTER FOURTEEN

A Constant Among Change

DOLLY CONSIDERED THE MOORES her parents. Dolly was saved at a Youth for Christ rally at the Mel Trotter Mission and often sang in the Mission services. When she married Paul Sullivan, Rev. Claude Moore performed the ceremony.

As organist for the Mission, I called the Moores Mammie and Pappie, and they called me their darling daughter. So it was with sadness that Dolly and I said good-bye to the Moores.

After only a few years, they returned to Minneapolis to take over the work of the Union City Rescue Mission. Paul, Dolly, and I kept in touch with them and often celebrated Christmas with the Moores. Claude and Grace later retired to Winona Lake and then moved to Orlando, Florida.

Mrs. Moore eventually became quite frail, and Mr. Moore patiently and sweetly cared for her. Then suddenly he was called home to be with the Lord, and Mrs. Moore was placed in a nursing home before she, several years later, joined her husband in glory. I'm sure that when they reached heaven they had an abundant entrance, and great will be their reward for their faithfulness in serving the Lord through so many years.

When the Moores left the Mel Trotter Mission in 1953, the Lord provided a ready replacement. In 1951,

Rev. John Kershaw had, for a short time, served as interim superintendent. He had worked out a monthly schedule for local churches and other Christian organizations to be responsible for meetings in the main Mission. Rev. George Bontekoe was one of the most frequent speakers on that schedule, and in February 1953, George became superintendent of the Mission. A native of Grand Rapids, he was educated in Christian schools and graduated from Christian High School. He received his Bible school training at the Moody Bible Institute in Chicago, and following his graduation served four churches in New York state.

In spite of changes in leadership and personnel, the Mission experienced reassuring constants. One was the annual Bible conference. At the 1954 conference, Homer Hammontree, still going strong, served as director of music, and, according to Homer, 1954 saw "one of the best conferences since Mel Trotter's homegoing."

Other constants were the calling ministry and the radio ministry, which allowed the Mission to reach into literally thousands of homes. The supporters, too, of the Mel Trotter Mission stood by the ministry and gave generously to keep the Old Lighthouse going. Volunteers gave time, effort, money, and clothing. And, of course, they uttered many prayers for the work of the Mission.

Other constants were not so reassuring. Skid row kept growing. Grand Rapids, the city of churches, still had many homes broken by divorce, quarreling, and sin—many homes were still unreached by the gospel.

Men and women—young and old—walked the street where the Branch Mission was located. The primary objective of that ministry was to present Jesus Christ to lost men and women. It was not the task of the staff to bring every person to Christ, but it was their privilege and responsibility to bring Christ to every person.

To accomplish that, gospel meetings were held every

night. Numerous local churches sent groups to the Mission to present the claims of Christ. After each service, soup was served in the basement for those who were hungry. When the men had finished eating, those who desired lodging were taken upstairs. Before going to bed, they were required to take a shower and to check all personal items—tobacco, matches, and loose change—then their clothing was placed in a fumigator (delouser) for about an hour.

In 1953, ten men were residing at the Branch Mission. Those men showed a real desire to be helped both materially and spiritually. They received three meals a day, shelter, and clothing. Bible classes were held for the men three nights a week. Those who worked at the Branch Mission believed that the Word of God held—and still holds—the only answer to the problems that the lost face.

Roy Hallam would have agreed that God's Word was the answer for him. "Nine months ago, I was a drunken sinner," he said. "Drink was my god. I had to have my drinks regardless of the cost. I found out the cost was heavy. It cost me the love of my wife and children. It cost me a happy home. It cost me jobs, money, and friends." It would have cost Roy his soul if he had not found Christ.

"I thank God for a mother who prayed for me, though I caused her many a heartache. She had to ask me to leave the house because I was causing so much trouble. Still she prayed that God would save her son."

One night, Roy staggered into the Branch Mission. "I was whipped—I mean, whipped by God. He had brought me down to the place where I saw myself as He saw me, rotten and filthy through and through, a sinner needing Christ as my Savior."

Roy called upon God with a repentant heart. "He saved me, 'For whosoever shall call upon the name of the Lord shall be saved,' and 'the blood of Jesus Christ his Son cleanseth us from all sin.'"

Roy's mother had been constant in prayer for her son, and she had the privilege of seeing God answer her prayers before she passed away. "Today I am happy in Jesus. As I walk by the beer taverns and see men and women soaked up in drink, I can look to Jesus and say, 'Thank you, Lord, for saving me.'"

Roy's two daughters, who at one time hated him, are now saved. They saw how Jesus had worked in Roy's life. "My daughter Esther said, 'Daddy, if the Lord can save you and change your life, He can do it for me also.' God brought her out of sin and confusion and now she is trusting in Christ."

Roy is a living testimony that it's wonderful to be saved and know that your life is shining for Jesus.

While the Branch Mission made changes in the lives of the men and women who entered there, the Mission itself experienced a change. Don Price became the assistant superintendent in charge of the Branch Mission. Don was born in Indianapolis and had lived for some time in Michigan. In Don, the down-and-outs who entered the Branch Mission found someone with whom they could relate. He was saved while serving time in an Indiana prison. After finding Christ, Don received his training at the Grand Rapids School of the Bible and Music.

Meanwhile, at the main Mission, Superintendent Bontekoe led the work. The summer work was especially fruitful at both locations. During August, nineteen men professed Christ in the Kent County Jail, and during September, twenty-one men professed Christ at the Branch Mission. Also during September, the Branch served 1,540 meals and provided 426 free lodgings.

But citing statistics does not relate the stories of heartache, sin, and misery. An incident occurred one Monday in March that illustrates that anything could happen at the Mission—and usually did. By 1954, a family Mission had been established at 60 Market Street where, as its name implies, families in trouble came for assistance. Lloyd Anderson, a young man who lived at the Mission with his wife, worked at the desk on Monday and Friday evenings. He answered the telephone and greeted those who came in "just to look the place over."

A very ragged and dirty man stumbled into the family Mission. "Where can I get a bed?" he said in a thick voice.

Lloyd looked the man over and felt strongly led to talk to him about the condition of his soul. Lloyd handed the man a gospel tract and talked to him about the unsearchable riches of Jesus Christ. The man's eyes darted back and forth between Lloyd's face and the tract. Suddenly, he crushed the tract into a ball and threw it into Lloyd's face; then he stormed out of the Mission.

Lloyd stood in the doorway and, in silence, watched the man leave. Larry Hall, who had witnessed the exchange, stood nearby. Lloyd turned to Larry and said, "There goes a fellow who is really under conviction."

No sooner had Lloyd spoken than the man lurched back into the Mission. Only this time there were tears in his eyes. He looked at Lloyd and said, "Man, I need something more than just a bed. I need help."

Lloyd then and there had the privilege of leading that man, Robert Howser, to the Lord Jesus Christ. And the funny thing is that Robert never did take the bed for which he came! March began in a wonderful way for Lloyd Anderson, but *life* began for Robert Howser, a sinner saved by grace.

Also by 1954, services were being held in the Kent County Jail every Sunday morning. Every Sunday for several weeks in a row that year, someone accepted Jesus Christ as Lord. One young man was detained for trial on charges of first-degree murder. He had been in and out of trouble for most of his young life, and he had a reputation as a hard guy.

One Sunday morning, in spite of himself, he listened to the testimonies of the men who represented the Mel Trotter Mission—ministers Allen, Scott, Hall, and Puls, among many others who serve in the jail work. As they told of the power of God to change people's lives, regardless of how tough or weak they might be, the young man's heart cried out for the need of a Savior. One of the personal workers who moved from cell to cell during the service came by just at the right time and led this young man to the One who could cleanse him from all of his unrighteousness. God truly poured out His richest blessings on the work in the jail.

On-site ministries were only a small part of the work. So large did the outreach ministries of the Mel Trotter Mission grow that during 1953 it became necessary to add two staff members. Their work consisted principally of calling.

Other staff members as well were added in 1954. John Rader came on as full-time assistant to Superintendent Bontekoe at the Main Mission, and Lawrence Hail was transferred to the Branch Mission as Don Price's assistant.

While God rescued souls through the work of the Mission, on a day in 1954 the main building of the Mel Trotter Mission itself became imperiled. One windy day, the sound of sirens startled Mission staff. The old Bixby Building next to the Mission had caught fire! As the Mission workers stood on the street out of harm's way, many whispering a few prayers, they feared that the Mission might also burn. They tested the wind and, with relief, noted that it was to the east, blowing away from the Mission. No sooner was the fire under control, however, than the wind turned to the west. Had the wind direction changed a short time earlier, there would likely have been no Mel Trotter Mission at 60 Market Street.

The Old Lighthouse was spared, but the building sustained considerable water damage. There would be difficult choices in the days ahead—what to save, what to let go.

But the evening of the fire, the Mission staff showed gratitude to God and to the firefighters by serving coffee to the men of the police and fire departments. Letters of appreciation for this ministry were sent by the police chief, the fire chief, and Mayor George Veldman, who wrote, "On behalf of the City of Grand Rapids, I want to thank you for the fine assistance your organization rendered at the Bixby fire. I was a personal observer for over two hours. It is this kind of neighborliness that makes our city such a wonderful place in which to live."

The damage to the Mission building was disheartening as the Mission workers contemplated the love and labor that had gone into turning the old structure from a hellhole into a haven. But no institution can live for long on the glory of her past. They were ready to move forward, accepting the challenge of the present hour.

It is ironic that in times of a strong economy there can be so many needs. In 1954, the country was experiencing a boom time, but there was still a strong demand for the Mel Trotter Mission ministries. Drinking, gambling, vice, and violence appeared to be on the increase, the products of which are seen in broken hearts, broken lives, broken bodies, and broken homes. These are the conditions with which a rescue mission deals, and God's grace has ever been the only answer.

In 1955, the Mel Trotter Branch Mission was constant in declaring the gospel of the grace of God to men and women on skid row. The Branch served a meal each night after the service. Then the workers sought to help people, rehabilitating them after they were born again.

The Branch also provided shelter for those with no place to go. In addition to a Bible class each Monday, Wednesday, and Friday, the Branch held a service every night of the week.

And, as ever, the goal of the Mel Trotter Mission was to turn people, even those deep in the valley of sin and shame, to the Lord Jesus Christ. But contrary to what one might expect, these lost people were not always strangers to the Word of God. A survey taken at the Mission showed that the greater percentage of the people who came to the Mission had experienced religious training and a better-than-average education. They had become victims, however, of the Archenemy of souls, and they had become weary travelers down a road of sin toward the campground of the dead. The Rescue Mission was for such as these.

To some, the call to salvation came too late. They laughed bitterly, standing a few moments perhaps outside the window of the Mission, then walked on into the shadows. But many, many others heard the gospel call and were washed in the precious blood of the Lamb.

As 1955 drew to a close, the Mission workers celebrated those converts and looked ahead to the new year—and to yet another annual Bible conference. Among the speakers were Dr. M. R. De Haan, founder and teacher of the *Radio Bible Class,* and Dr. Bob Jones Jr., president of Bob Jones University in Greenville, South Carolina.

Music for the conference was again under the direction of Homer Hammontree, who had directed the conference music for at least thirty years. Ham and the Rescue Mission's founder, Mel Trotter, were for years the closest of friends. Fifteen years earlier Ham had bid farewell to his friend, and soon he would be bidding farewell to another symbol of rescue work in the city of Grand Rapids.

David Zylstra Remembers

My first recollection of the Mel Trotter Mission was when I was around twelve years of age. I went to a Saturday afternoon Bible class with about three hundred other kids. Mr. Trotter was in charge of the preliminaries. He was always cheerful, an excellent emcee with a rotund belly.

Then later, the City Rescue Mission had a week of evangelistic meetings with excellent, well-known speakers. Casey Vander Jagt would usually be present and, at the appropriate time, would break in with an "Amen, brother!"

I have many fond memories of the Mel Trotter Mission. The focus has changed, but its purpose is the same—to bring people to Jesus Christ, nurture them in the faith, and make their faith a vital part of their everyday lives.

ぴ CHAPTER FIFTEEN

The Light Still Shines

THE OLD LIGHTHOUSE WAS SOLD. One can imagine the stunned expressions as Mission workers and supporters read the news in the *Mission Messenger*. But it had been no secret that the old building had long since become more of a liability than an asset. It had become an increasing financial burden, and quite unexpectedly the opportunity arose to dispose of it advantageously.

Torn between sentiment for the past and the desire to cut costs by providing modern facilities under one roof, the board, after study and prayer, decided to sell.

When Mel Trotter first looked over the old Smith Opera House and saloon, it was located in the very center of a cesspool of sin and iniquity—a red-light district, no less—a state of affairs that, due to the Mission's ministry, had ceased to exist. The ministry was then directed away to other areas, eventually bringing about the opening of the Branch Mission, where on-the-spot rescue work could be performed.

With the savings effected through greater efficiency in building maintenance, heating and lighting, and time saved by the centralization of staff members' work, it was believed that the Mission work could be both broadened and intensified. As the result of this change, many more souls could be saved, which was, after all, the purpose of the ministry.

The *Grand Rapids Press* made an announcement under a picture of the historic former opera house: "Landmark Bows to Parking Push." The article, titled "From Souls to Sedans", stated that "the four-story structure at 60 Market Avenue, N.W., built in 1885 as the Smith Opera House and for fifty years the home of the Mel Trotter Mission, would be making way for a two-story parking ramp."

From hellhole to haven to parking lot. It was natural at that time to do some reminiscing. The Mission had a glorious history. Many, many people had been saved at its altar; many people had been blessed by its Bible-teaching ministry; and some of those people had gone from its doors to full-time gospel ministry. It would be hard to estimate the Mission's influence for God upon this community. Had there never been a Rescue Mission, Grand Rapids would have been the poorer spiritually.

But one cannot live in the past. If Mel Trotter himself had been living, he no doubt would have made the move sooner. He would not have been concerned with sentiment or consideration for his own personality. The man who coined the phrase "everlastingly at it" moved three times his first six years in Grand Rapids so that he might improve the opportunities to reach the lost for Christ.

The sale of the old Mission building was thus an auspicious start for George Bontekoe's third year as superintendent at the Mission. "It has been a busy and blessed three years," said George. "There have been hard things as well as pleasant things. But all in all, it has been a joy to be of service, especially to those who are up against it."

George would be the first to admit that rescue mission work is not easy, and he was aware that the coming year, with the move to a new location, would be hard.

"Our prayer," he said, "is that in the midst of all these changes, we may have continued strength and wisdom. But above all, pray that we may have power with God and power with men."

It was apparent that the Mission work did, indeed, exhibit power through its many ministries, including the Branch Mission. One Saturday night, a young man passed the Branch Mission. Music was going out over the loudspeaker, and it gripped the heart of the young man. He was drunk. In his arms was his little baby, who had been placed there by his wife. She thought the presence of the baby would keep him out of a beer joint.

"I was looking for a place to ditch the baby," said Fred Mason, "when I heard the gospel music from the Mission." The Holy Spirit drew Fred inside the building.

Don Price, the Branch Mission superintendent, gave Fred a seat in the back of the room. "I noticed that he was crying," said Don, "and that he was under deep conviction of sin. I asked him to go downstairs with me where I could deal with him from the Word of God and show him how to be saved."

Don's wife held the baby, and after Don talked with the young man, Fred said that he would like to receive the Lord Jesus Christ as his Savior, but he would like for his wife to do so at the same time. "The next day," said Don, "we went to Fred's house, and there led him and his wife, Patsy, to the Lord." Fred, Patsy, and their four children became established in one of the local churches. One cannot help but wonder: what if Fred had not heard the gospel music from the Mission that night?

It was vital that the work of the Mel Trotter Mission not be interrupted during the period of move and change. To that end, the Heyman Building on Monroe Avenue, almost directly opposite the Branch Mission, was leased as temporary quarters for the Main Mission. Shortly thereafter, something unusual happened.

"A man about sixty years old walked into the Branch by mistake," said Rev. Bontekoe. "He thought, so he said, that he was walking into a beer joint. Don Price introduced him to the Water of Life. He has not as yet accepted Him, but he left us his home address."

Across the street at the Heyman location, someone stopped to pick up bedding and baby clothes for a mother and child deserted by the husband and father of the home. The next day, the Mission sent them a cot for the child, cooking utensils, and food.

It's a needy world—a challenge for the outreach ministries. With that in view, Eleanor Tuinstra was added to the staff. Her work consisted largely of calling on the unchurched of the Mission neighborhood.

Once the Mission was settled into its temporary housing in the Heyman Building, property was purchased that would become the permanent Mission headquarters. The Kent Theater and Oaks Hotel properties, both on Monroe Avenue across from the Heyman Building, would become the Mission's new home.

Substantial repairs and improvements were needed on those properties, the cost of which would run to more than sixty thousand dollars. That, however, would be borrowed and repaid out of funds to be received over a fifteen-year period from the sale of the old Mission property.

It would not be necessary to ask the friends of the Mission for financial help in the purchase and improvement of the new home for the Old Lighthouse. None of the building funds, however, could be used for operating expenses. It was gratifying, indeed, that God's children gave generously to keep the doors open and the gospel going out to the lost. This is the best report that the Mission could give to its friends: souls are being saved.

A month later, remarkable changes had taken place

to the old Kent Theater, which became the Mission's new auditorium. The former Oaks Hotel was turned into offices, with room for a Sunday school, sewing circle, auxiliary, prayer meetings, and the various other meetings associated with the Mission.

In October 1956, the Mission headquarters moved from its temporary site in the Heyman Building across the street to the new offices. Homer Hammontree said, "As the dear old Mission has a new home, may it have the greatest ministry of its whole life. Why not? God is able! May He grant it for His own name's sake."

Homer was right. The Old Lighthouse would shine no matter what street it happened to sit on. The year of 1956—even with all of its opportunities—still challenged the Mission work as never before. Men and women still needed to be saved, and the Mission still had a place to fill in the spiritual life of the city.

The Lord was surely with the Mission work in its new location. Many people passed the doors every day—people who needed the Savior. And the workers were glad when people stopped in, for they found it a pleasure to point these people to Jesus Christ.

The Mission continued its varied ministries, its beacon fanning out over the community. Not only was the street population reached nightly through the Branch services but also families were ministered to. Not only were services conducted in the new chapel and auditorium but also the radio ministry reached out daily. The Mel Trotter Mission was an arm of the church, supplementing a kind of work not usually done by the churches.

On October 18–21, 1956, the Mission held official dedication celebrations at the new permanent site, and the Christmas letter to the friends of the Mission from the board and staff included a message from their hearts: "What a year this has been! Our hearts are filled to overflowing when we ponder the doings of our God in our midst. We repeat again and again, What hath God wrought! The impossible has been accomplished over and over again before our very eyes. Only God can do the impossible. How can we help but love Him?"

The best way for the Mission to proclaim the love of God was to continue in His work. And the Mission's work for the year began in 1957, as it had every year since 1900, with the annual Bible conference.

Superintendent Bontekoe, in an impassioned statement, addressed the conference in the new facilities: "Relocating the Main Mission puts the total work right in the midst of an area of great need. How I wish you could feel the heartthrob of those who have been caught in a web of sin and trouble. It would be a spiritual experience you would not soon forget. It would send you to your homes thankful for God's goodness to you. And it would send you to your knees to pray more than ever for the ministry of rescue missions."

The first of February 1957 marked the beginning of Superintendent Bontekoe's fifth year with the Mission, a year that witnessed a change in the Saturday night schedule. Youth for Christ decided to return to the Ladies Literary Club auditorium for its meetings. The Mission auditorium would be used for ministering to the people who came to lower Monroe Avenue for their Saturday night fun and for reaching them with the gospel.

Those who entered the Mission buildings would find a more modern exterior. Remodeling plans for the Branch Mission included a new front on the two Monroe Avenue buildings, making the two into one. When the remodeling was completed, there were two new offices, a new air-conditioned chapel, a large prayer room, a new dining room, a new dishwashing room with modern equipment, a ladies restroom, a new shower room on the third floor, and a new clothing room in the basement.

With the new facilities, the Mission building had a

more workable floor plan than ever before. "God has done great and wonderful things for us here at the Old Lighthouse," said George Bontekoe, "both at the Main and the Branch Missions, whereof we are glad. We pray that we shall be faithful in using all of the facilities God has given us for one supreme purpose—to reach the lost for Christ."

The Mission dedicated the remodeled Branch Mission on October 5 and 6, 1957. An open house at the Branch for those two days gave visitors an opportunity to see what the Lord had done.

That you never know what unexpected things the Lord may do is as true today as it was in 1958. In the five and a half years George Bontekoe had been superintendent of the Mel Trotter Mission, he had seen a lot of needy people.

"I remember the drinking doctor," said George, "the distraught lawyer, the one-time business executive, the erring father whose daughter was a missionary, the alcoholic women, the women of easy virtue, the children from broken homes, the runaways, the young people who were at odds with the law, and a host of others that would be classed as ordinary citizens."

One never knows who might come through the door of a mission. One cannot accurately judge people by their clothes; neither can one accurately judge people by their looks.

Anyway, what difference does it make? We have to look beyond the clothes, beyond the unshaven face, and beyond the liquor-laden breath. We have, first of all, to see the heart-need of a person. Everyone everywhere needs Jesus Christ the Lord. The high, the low, the rich, and the poor have this in common—they need Christ the Savior.

Our first duty is to tell people of the change that Christ can make on the inside—in the heart. People need more than a change of circumstances or a change of environment. The need is deeper than that! A person needs a cleansed heart, a new standard of values, a new sense of direction, and the power of God to carry through. When men and women accept Jesus Christ as their personal Lord and Savior, they have all of that—and more. When the change of heart is real, the change of circumstances usually follows.

Over the decade of the fifties, the Mel Trotter Mission witnessed many turns of events in its own circumstances. The decade began with several changes in interim superintendents, saw new programs and classes added, and witnessed the end of an era with the demolition of the old Mission headquarters.

As the fifties drew to a close, the Mission staff looked back over the history of the Mel Trotter Mission and celebrated fifty-nine years of spreading the gospel of Jesus Christ—forty years of it under the leadership of Melvin E. Trotter.

During all of that time, the responsibility of the Mission was to minister, especially to the unreached and needy of our city. And throughout that period the constant support of the Mission work had been the living God, who upheld us and the many ministries through interested people, groups, churches, and businesses. For the decades ahead, the Mission planned to continue—to carry on faithfully and to expand the God-given ministry until Jesus comes again.

Throughout the history of the Old Lighthouse, it had been blessed with capable, dynamic men directing its beacon. But the Mission also succeeded through the work of self-confident and energetic women. In October 1959, the Mission had on staff many such women. These were ordinary women, really, but ordinary women who shone with their own special light and whom God had used in extraordinary ways.

Anna Smith taught the adult women's Sunday school class, a group who met every Sunday afternoon for Bible study.

Eleanor Tuinstra served as the Mission's family worker and taught the young mothers' Sunday school class. This group also met once a month in the various homes of the members to help young mothers both spiritually and socially.

Miss Tuinstra also visited the women in the Kent County Jail and wrote to and visited with some of the women of the Detroit House of Correction. She also visited the homes of many people, bringing as she went the message of Jesus Christ and the blessings of a helping hand.

Mrs. M. Furgerson headed the Women's Fellowship on Sunday afternoons. Missionary speakers addressed the ladies, and, following an inspirational session, they enjoyed supper together.

Mrs. Stanley Stapley directed the Tuesday Sewing Circle. Mending, making sheets, quilting, and canning (850 quarts that year) were some of the tasks that these ladies performed.

Chris Hartoog was president of the Women's Auxiliary. Once a month, they enjoyed a potluck dinner followed by devotions, mission reports, an offering, special music, and a speaker. In addition to towels, food, and other supplies, this group bought various pieces of equipment for the Mission.

Eleanor Tuinstra, Mrs. G. Buning, and Mary Burman shared responsibility for the Thursday afternoon Bible class. This class met twice a month and was composed of mothers who came for the clothing that was distributed following the meeting.

Mrs. Hershell Sigler served as the Mission's office secretary. She was generally the first to greet the transient woman or the stranded family who came to the Mission for help.

Not only, then, did the Mission minister to women, but also many women found the Mission a place where they could serve the Lord. God bless them.

Testimony of H. A. Berry

The Mel Trotter Mission is especially dear to me, for it was there that I came to know the Lord Jesus Christ as my personal Savior on October 12, 1935.

I came into the Mission that Monday night utterly discouraged and at the end of the road. Mel Trotter brought the message that night, and as I listened, the words sank into my troubled, discouraged heart. I realized that here at last was the answer to all my needs and problems. That the Lord Jesus Christ took my sins and bore them in His own body on the tree that He might offer me a pardon full and free seemed too good to be true.

I went forward when the invitation was given, and there, kneeling at the altar, I prayed the penitent's prayer, acknowledged my utter unworthiness, and humbly accepted the gracious gift of salvation through Jesus Christ, our sin-bearer. And truly, I was born again, for my life changed completely. I had the sweet assurance I was now His child and sweet peace became my balm. I now had Someone who could help me, and He has been my Helper in all of life's journey all these years since I gave my heart to Him.

The Lord Jesus is indeed precious to me. I praise God for the Mel Trotter Mission, a lighthouse shining for God, giving out the sweet gospel story that Jesus saves and keeps and satisfies.

ᶜᶠ CHAPTER SIXTEEN

Investments in Love

WHAT'S THE USE? THAT IS THE philosophy of skid row. It is a philosophy of hopelessness and despair. Life is not easy for the homeless and transient. They have experienced failure, defeat, and rejection. Life for them has become a matter of drifting from city to city, landing in and out of jail, getting drunk and drying out, trying to forget, and always running away. Many of these people want to be forgotten—left to their lives of misery.

Into this picture comes the Mel Trotter Mission with its message of Calvary and Calvary's love. The gospel of the Lord Jesus Christ is the only message of hope for the lost. God's love for even the lowest of humanity is evidenced in the lives of those who meet, serve, and counsel with lost sinners at the Mission in the heart of western Michigan.

The Mel Trotter Mission is a haven, too, for the teen-ager who has run away from home and does not want to return to his drinking father; for the mother of small children who has no heat for her home and no husband to help her with the problem; for the man who comes in barefoot—and another who has only rubbers on his feet; and for the hungry, the distraught, the sin-sick, the lonely, the alcoholic, and the homeless parolee.

All sorts of needs presented themselves constantly at the Mission doors. And, just as it had in 1900, the Mission did its best in the sixties—under God—to invest lives with hope.

The January 1960 annual Bible conference remained a constant, with Homer Hammontree again serving as musician. That year, the Christian High School choir performed a Saturday night concert.

And there was something new for 1960—special Bible class meetings taught by Dr. William "Billy" McCarrell, pastor of the Cicero, Illinois, Bible Church. The purpose of these Bible classes was to help defeated people discover the resources for victory offered by God's Word through Jesus Christ. Many people who came to the Mission for help had little or no knowledge of the great power of God. Many had lived in deep sin for a long time. It was hoped that in these meetings the Spirit of God would, through the ministry of Dr. McCarrell and the Word of God, bring many of these people into a life of spiritual victory and stability.

The annual Bible conference of 1961 brought to mind the many years that I served as organist for the conferences. I recall that, when I was a little girl, my mother had taken me to these meetings, then held in the old opera house. I always sat in the front row of the balcony on the side where the piano stood. I sometimes leaned over so far that my mother would grab my coat and say, "If you lean much farther, you're going to land in that man's lap."

Little did I imagine that one day I would be a part of that great program. The first time that I participated in the conference was shortly after my mother went to be with the Lord. I remember wanting to tell her, "Look, Mom. Can you see what I'm doing?" I think that she did.

Other workers at the Mission could also look back fondly. One of the desk clerks, the cook, the dining room man, the clothing room manager, the dish room man, and the squad leader of our clean-up gang were all saved at the Mel Trotter Mission.

The Mission was the site of saved souls among young people, too. The Grand Rapids Youth for Christ was again meeting at the Mission auditorium. For a time they had been meeting at the St. Cecilia auditorium. Tedd Bryson, director of the Grand Rapids Youth for Christ, wrote about the way God had blessed his ministry: "Just a short word of appreciation for the past season. We certainly thank you for making the Mel Trotter auditorium available to us Saturday nights. Since the first of January, 392 young people have made decisions as a result of the ministry of Youth for Christ. About two hundred of these have taken place during our Saturday night rallies in your auditorium. Certainly God has used your facilities to enhance our ministry."

The year 1961 held sad news, too. "On July 29, after a brief illness," said superintendent Rev. George Bontekoe in the August 1961 *Mission Messenger*, "God called to His heavenly home my beloved wife. The loss is great and keenly felt. So often, her word of encouragement and wisdom was just what I, her preacher husband, needed."

Then, his sorrow was doubled. For on August 6, 1961, God called Rev. Bontekoe's mother home. She had been sick for some time, and although her going was not unexpected, it did indeed increase the superintendent's grief.

"Hearing her testimony of faith and assurance, as she lay upon her bed of illness," said Rev. Bontekoe, "is something the family will not soon forget. During most of her years she enjoyed good health and strength, and she used that strength to do her very best for her family. Although we all loved Mother and truly miss her, we know she has gone to be with Jesus. This greatly comforts us, for we know that 'to depart, and to be with Christ is far better' than anything earth offers."

The Mission in the sixties reached many people with the gospel of the Lord Jesus Christ, and some of them heard the call of God to Christian service. Others, through the Bible classes at the annual conferences, came to a greater knowledge of and love for the Word of God.

The first of February 1963 marked the beginning of Rev. Bontekoe's eleventh year as superintendent of the Mel Trotter Mission. And soon he had something else to celebrate. Miss Eleanor Tuinstra had served faithfully in the Mission and had been a real asset to the work. On April 6, 1963, the *Mission Messenger* announced the marriage of Eleanor Tuinstra and George Bontekoe.

It's no surprise that Rev. Bontekoe did not speak the next evening at the Mission's regular Sunday evening service on April 7. Filling in for him was a familiar figure—Casey Vander Jagt, evangelist, saved under Mel Trotter's ministry. Casey, a converted taxi driver who had specialized in finding "a good time" for his fares, reminded us of the wonderful workings of God. The Mission would soon experience more wonders.

The sixties were a time of social upheaval—the sexual revolution, increased drug use, sexually transmitted diseases, and distrust by young people for established institutions, including the church. Thus, at that time in its history, the Mission turned its focus on young people, children, and families.

Just as the Mission was deciding how best to implement its new ideas, Mr. and Mrs. Hale J. MacKay invested in the Mission's new focus by donating to the Mel Trotter Mission a twenty-one thousand dollar brick and block building at 704 Jefferson Avenue S.E. This building was wonderfully suited for children and young people. It had a chapel with a seating capacity of sixty persons, a recreation area, and four Sunday school rooms. On the first Sunday of meetings in that new facility, an eleven-year-old boy accepted Jesus as his Savior.

The new site thus became home to a ministry for the families of the community. Gospel services, Sunday school, a children's Bible club, Pioneer Girls and Awana Boys clubs, a meeting for mothers, and a midweek Bible study all were held there.

After a few months in operation in the new building, the work was both fruitful and difficult. Our best Sunday evening attendance so far was a respectable forty-five, but discipline presented a problem in the children's programs. Those who worked there looked upon the neighborhood as a gold mine of opportunity, but there was much need of prayer. One wonders if it was purely coincidence that Frank Peck, head of the jail workers' group, was given general oversight of the work at 704 Jefferson.

The 1966 annual Bible conference marked the halfway point of the sixties. And it marked, as well, a giant void in the music program. Homer Hammontree went to be with the Lord. Homer had been with Mel Trotter during the days of their ministry to the soldiers of World War I, and he had been associated with the Mission for almost fifty years.

Homer's homegoing seemed like the passing of an institution, and that same year witnessed yet another change for the Mission. The urban renewal programs of the sixties displaced the headquarters on Monroe Avenue. The Lord—as always—was with us, however, and the Mel Trotter Mission found a new home—the old Salvation Army building on Commerce Avenue.

As is sometimes the case, blessing can be mixed. To meet health standards and building codes, the structure required extensive remodeling, which placed a strain on the Mission budget. But on Sunday, October 20, 1968, the Mel Trotter Mission held a special dedication and open house at the new Commerce Avenue building.

Many people in attendance at the ceremonies couldn't help but think back over the history of this most essential and important ministry—one that had served as an arm of the church for sixty-eight years. The original Mission in 1900 was first located on Canal Street. Its founder, Mel Trotter—who served as superintendent for forty years—oversaw four hundred professions of faith made during the Mission's first year.

From that time on there were many moves and several new superintendents, but the Mission continued to increase in outreach: a daily radio program, jail ministry, Sunday school, nightly evangelistic meetings, women's fellowship, Pioneer Girls, Boys' Clubs, women's auxiliary, Maranatha Men's Luncheon every Thursday noon, Bible clubs, and family work. The Mission truly had invested its message of God's love throughout the community.

Although social norms and attitudes shift, human needs remain the same. And the needs of the sixties were much the same as those of the 1900s. The police department still asked, "Will you feed a stranded couple?" The hospital inquired, "Will you provide lodging for a stranger who has come in for emergency treatment?" A social agency wanted to know, "What can you do to help a homeless family of six?"

Many fine agencies in the city could help people such as these, but not all agencies were open twenty-four hours a day. The Mission, too, is more than an agency. People need more than physical and material help. Their never-dying souls need help, too. The Mission gives the gospel to those who seek its help, and thus the Mission is a soul-winning arm of the church.

At the close of the sixties, the men's division served as an example of time and effort well spent. It ministered to the needs in every area of a man's life—shelter, food, clothing, medical care, job opportunities, and personal counseling. Spiritual need is, of course, uppermost in the thinking of the Mission, so every night of the year a gospel service was conducted by a different church group or Christian organization. Transient men from every part of the country could be found in attendance.

Some men resided at the Mission indefinitely. They had professed faith in Christ and were involved in a rehabilitation program that was designed to build them up in every possible way.

For almost seventy years, the Mel Trotter Mission had been reaching a helping hand to distressed people. That is where Christ puts the emphasis, and that is a good place for the investment of effort, time, prayers, and gifts.

***

Testimony of William R. Bennett

I was brought up in a Christian home. In the fall of 1938, a young man invited me to attend a young people's meeting at the Mel Trotter Mission. I became so interested in Bible study that I began attending every Thursday, and then every Friday at the citywide Bible class.

It wasn't long until I saw something that I had never seen before—men and women being born again. I observed them as they would leave their sinful lives and take on a new life with Christ.

On the thirtieth of January 1939, I was singing with a choir of young people during an evangelistic campaign conducted by Dr. Amy Lee Stockton and Rita Gould at the old Mel Trotter Mission on Market Street. As the service progressed, the thought was going through my mind, *Bill, what if you died tonight?*

When Miss Stockton gave the invitation, she said, "If there is the slightest doubt in your mind that you are saved, you should move forward tonight." There was doubt in my mind. A voice seemed to say, "Bill, why don't you get it settled tonight?"

I failed to go forward. When I reached home, the only private place to pray was the bathroom. There, I locked the door, fell to my knees, and asked God to show me whether or not I was saved.

A voice said, "Bill, haven't I said in my Word that if you believe, you will be saved?" I said, "Yes, Lord, but what does it mean to believe?"

Then I saw a vision of Jesus hanging on the cross. I could see the crown of thorns, the blood flowing from His hands, His feet, and His side. Then a voice said, "Bill, this is what I did for you. I paid the price for your salvation. I took your place. Eternal life is a gift. You can't pay for it, nor can you earn it. Neither can you obtain it by just living a good life."

The joy of my life today is telling of His saving and keeping power. God called me into His service as superintendent of the Haven of Rest Rescue Mission of Bristol, Virginia. He has given me a wonderful helpmate whom I met while helping in the work of the Mel Trotter Mission, and He has given us two fine children, both Christians.

Camping Out with God

THE MISSION HAD A NEW DREAM. Grand Rapids had become a city of ethnic diversity, and for a number of years the superintendent and the board were concerned about reaching boys and girls from all ethnic groups. With the onset of the seventies, the Mission felt an urgent need. The Lord loves every human being, and the Mission is called to serve each one. Thus, all boys and girls are precious—the hope of our nation's future. We began to pray for a camp.

The Mission needed land—land with trees—where we could provide programs during the summer and on weekends all year long. The dream included a shelter, a pool, and facilities to establish a day camp. It also included busing for children and mothers from the inner city to give them an experience away from squalor and a chance to hear that God loves them.

Dreams and prayers are a start, but God also expects us to take action. As a first step to reaching the young people, a youth director was added to the staff. He would work in the Sunday school, Pioneer Girls, Boys' Service Brigade, and other club work. While involved in the usual Mission work, he would at the same time formulate plans for a year-round day-camp program.

Meanwhile, the Mission continued to reach young people through the programs that were already in operation—and through their parents. Jim and Doris Ross had been attending the Sunday evening evangelistic meetings, the Friday night Bible class, the Tuesday night prayer service, and the annual Bible conferences. The whole Ross family had been regular in attendance, too, at a local church for many years. None of the Ross children, however, had ever been born again, which for Jim and Doris was a tremendous burden.

Then, at an invitation time at the Mission, their sixteen-year-old daughter made her way to the front and surrendered her life to Jesus Christ. A few weeks later, the film *No Need to Hide* was shown. At the invitation time following the film, the couple's thirteen-year-old daughter accepted Christ Jesus as her Savior. At a Tuesday night prayer meeting, both parents gave their testimonies and expressed gratitude to the Lord for the Mel Trotter Mission. Because of its role as an arm of the church, two of their children had been saved.

Testimonies about young people accepting Christ as Savior were a source of joy, but the experience of the Ross family made it apparent that young people needed to hear the full story of salvation. The Mission became more determined than ever to provide programs for children and young people through a camp. But with still no suitable site, other special programs were provided. Day camping, overnight camping, canoeing, fishing trips, picnics, and special excursions to Jack Wyrtzen's Word of Life Rally and to Bob Lo Island with twenty-two young people all proved to be most profitable to our Lord. As a result of these special events, many boys and girls made commitments to Christ.

Reaching boys and girls, as well as mothers and fathers, in the inner city was a challenge. Thus, the Mission stepped up its schedule of activities for the fall, winter, and spring months. The new schedule included a woodworking shop, basketball, winter sports, and hiking, as

well as an enlarged family work program. All of these programs would strengthen Christians and help many people
come to know Jesus as their personal Savior.

Although the Mission staff was grateful for every boy
and girl the Lord sent to the Mission, there were trials
and testing. Often, young people try to see what they
can get away with. But it was thrilling to watch them
come to know Christ as Savior and to witness their spiritual growth.

The Mission's ongoing programs for children and
young people, as well as its existing programs for adults,
consumed a lot of resources; yet, the Mission staff had
never stopped praying about a permanent camp. Then
toward the end of 1973, God allowed the Mission to
acquire a tract of land sufficient for day camping and
recreational programs.

The property was beautiful, located outside of Grand
Rapids about twenty-five miles from the Mission. It was
ideal for all types of sports activities. There were slopes
for skiing, sledding, and tobogganing; a wonderful valley and splendid wooded sections for hiking and wilder-
ness camping; and several nearby bodies of water for
canoeing and swimming.

The camp would be called Camp Mel-Tro-Mi, and
from the beginning there was thrilling evidence of the
Lord's approval of the Mission's project. Material sup-
pliers gave real discounts and, in some instances, made
substantial outright grants. An architect provided plans
for the building, and another company surveyed the land
at no charge. Several different contractors contributed
grading, installed footings, and erected walls—all at no
charge.

Day camp on our very own property was a new experience for the Mission staff, but everyone was eager to
hold programs at the campsite. Even before the facilities were completed, the Mission held activities out in

the open. The Lord provided beautiful weather, and the children enjoyed romping in the outdoors. Sixty youngsters, many of whom attended every day, benefited from not only the wholesome recreation but also the daily teaching of the Word.

Over the summer, the leaders became better acquainted with the children and their needs. All of the Mission staff had hoped and prayed that the day camp would contribute both to the children's physical and mental development and their growth in the things of the Lord.

While the children played under the trees, the all-purpose building took shape. Workers first laid the foundation then put in the plumbing. Next, they poured the cement floor. Finally, they put up the walls.

Next, the construction crew completed the service building at Camp Mel-Tro-Mi—at no cost to the Mission. The Mission staff was so grateful to those workers whom God had sent to help make this dream become a reality. Many wonderful people gave their time, material, and money to make the camp possible. With construction completed at a minimal demand on Mission resources, it would be possible to plan for six cabins for boys and girls.

By 1977, our Mel-Tro-Mi Youth Camp was reaching more than three hundred children with the gospel. Many of those children came from broken homes and were unloved and unwanted. They received concentrated attention and Bible instruction at the camp.

Meanwhile, the other Mission programs for young people were in full operation. Those programs, too, received generous support from the community. To make our cup run over, the downtown Kiwanis Club of Grand Rapids granted the Mission one thousand dollars with which to purchase mechanical equipment for our boys' workshop program.

The Boys' Club also saw fruits of the Mission's labor in Christ. Two boys in particular, Alex and Will, had been coming for five years, and they provided a real Christian testimony to the others in the Club. Alex and Will asked if they could help the younger boys in Bible memory work and at game time. The two young men discovered that they had a knack for teaching and leading, and they were gratified by the younger boys' appreciation of their help. As a result of that Boys' Club experience, Alex and Will talked about going to Bible college upon graduation from high school. The Mission started a fund to help them with their education, and the staff had the joy of knowing that the Lord had called two fine young men to study for a full-time ministry.

Witnessing the fruits of working with youngsters and knowing how the Lord worked in the lives of young people, the Mission staff would only smile when occasionally someone would ask, "In 1978, with its modern dilemmas, aren't youth programs and Bible camps like Mel-Tro-Mi passé?" The Mel Trotter Mission ministers regularly to about three hundred young people. The boys and girls who come to Mel-Tro-Mi Camp are loved, cared for, and have fun, but, above all, they are learning truths, precious facts of salvation that they will never forget. Passé? Young people such as Alex and Will discover the joy of learning, leading, and giving. During 1977 in the camp programs alone, several young people came to salvation, and many others asked for further information.

But the children are not the only ones who benefit from the youth programs. Sally, one of the counselors at Mel-Tro-Mi during the 1978 camp season, learned a lesson about prayer from one of the campers. Early in the week, Jane, one of the little girls, lost her mother's hairbrush.

"Jane cried as she recounted the story to me," said

Sally, "and then she asked if we could pray about it. All of the girls in the cabin joined in with prayers that day and the next, asking the Lord to help us find the brush." The girls also took action and searched the entire camp-grounds for the hairbrush. But by the end of the week the brush still hadn't been found.

Sally reassured the girls: "The Lord answers prayer, but in his own time." And sure enough, He did. By the following week, the missing hairbrush was found and returned to its owner.

Oh, that we at times could be more childlike, never doubting that God cares for every one of us. If God counts every hair on Jane's head, it follows that He takes account of even the smallest matters—even Jane's con-cern about her mother's lost hairbrush.

Rev. Robert D. McCarthy Remembers

On January 19, 1921, I accepted Christ at the old City Rescue Mission. It was the annual Bible conference, and Mel Trotter gave his life's story that night.

Because of the crowd, they asked the children to come down and sit on the platform steps to make room for others. I was nine years old.

As I listened and watched the tears run down Mr. Trotter's cheeks, I couldn't help but know that it was God's power that delivered him from the power of drink and sin. Even though I was just a kid, I thought, *If God could save a man like that, He can save and keep me from such a sad experience.*

I went forward just a few steps and knelt at the altar. Dr. Porter, a Christian dentist, knelt beside me and ex-plained the plan of salvation. Then he helped me to call on the Lord for salvation. We memorized John 5:24 on our knees that night before I went home.

Reach Out–I'll Be There

THE 1970S HAD BEEN FULL of blessings, and the *Mission Messenger* reported all of them. The newsletter was a way the Mission reached out to its many supporters, and it was printed by the Mission's own print shop. The newsletter was not, however, the only publication produced there.

Many supporters of the Mission wondered how the Mel Trotter Mission could afford to produce the many informational publications such as the *Mission Messenger,* tracts, bookmarks, place mats, church bulletins, letters, and all of the office forms.

By the 1970s, to save money, the Mission staff designed, printed, and addressed all of its informational material and its office forms in its own print shop. The history of the printing operation is a story in itself.

In the mid-1960s, the William B. Eerdmans Publishing Company had given the Mission some metal partitions, a gift that filled a real need. Then around 1970, the Interstate Motor Freight Company provided the Mission with several pieces of equipment: an addressograph plate-making and automatic addressing machine and a Multilith Offset Press with cabinets, frames, plates, and labels. The Steelcase Company made available some new cabinets, and, along with all of the equipment donated earlier by several businesses, the Mission added a trimmer, a folder, and a sealing machine.

After his retirement in 1974, Sid Stapley, whose parents so faithfully served in Mission work for many years, joined the Mel Trotter Mission staff. Sid did all of the printing—including all office record forms used in the various departments—on a part-time basis at a very low cost. A fine Christian gentleman, a member of the Mission Board of Directors, provided a large percentage of the paper at no cost.

And the Mission couldn't possibly handle the volume of mailing without the help of volunteers—about ten Christian women who, along with some of the staff (one receiving no salary), did all of the stuffing of envelopes for mailing.

Without the Lord's providing all of the equipment, workers, and volunteers, it would have been impossible to keep the friends and supporters of this ministry advised of the great things that the Lord was doing at the Mel Trotter Mission.

Included among the great events at the Mission was the diamond jubilee of this institution in 1975. That year also witnessed a change in leadership: George Bontekoe, superintendent for more than twenty years, left that position to became a chaplain. Henry Sonneveldt, for years part owner of the Sonneveldt Company, took over as interim superintendent. He had been a long-time member of the Mission Board of Directors, and he had known Mel Trotter personally.

Henry was a blessing to the ministry and had graciously stepped in to assume temporary leadership. But at the end of May 1976, it was time for him to step down, and the Mission had not yet found the right man to take over. Then, after much prayer and searching, the Board of Directors heard about a man, a real soul-winner who was well-known in Grand Rapids and surrounding areas as a man of God. Many people had attested to his loving concern for the lost and to the

fruitful ministry he had conducted for the Lord Jesus
Christ.

The Rev. Henry Hoekstra was a graduate of Reformed
Bible College in Grand Rapids and a former businessman
and resident of the area. He had been most effective in
developing new churches for the Christian Reformed
denomination. The Board of Directors and the staff
members were delighted to welcome Rev. Hoekstra as
their leader and new superintendent, effective September
15, 1976.

Other great things taking place in the 1970s included
some of the Mission's regular programs: the mail ministry, the men's lodging house, the women's ministry,
and the annual Bible conference.

The jail and prison ministry, which began in 1900,
required ever greater efforts by the 1970s. To serve better in the jail ministry, Lawrence Hall, director of the
jail and prison ministry, received his certificate from the
Michigan Sheriff's Association. His new badge gave him
entrance to any jail in the state that participated in this
program and privileges to visit any prisoner who re-
quested counseling. Sometimes it was necessary to take
clothing to prisoners for their court appearances.

The increased population of the institutions that the
jail ministry served provided both discouragement and
triumph. At one meeting, the men were particularly
unruly—so much so that the prison minister became
disheartened. During the following month, Mission staff
spent much time in prayer about the situation. At the
next scheduled meeting, the men were attentive, and at
the close of the service nine men came to Christ. It
seemed as though the Lord was saying, "Be faithful in
sowing the seed, and I will give the increase."

The men's lodging house, too, continued to reach out
and fill an ongoing need. During 1973, the men's lodging house provided 12,386 beds nightly, served 33,659

meals, gave away 3,430 items of clothing and shoes to needy men, and provided evening chapel services to 7,258 persons.

The Mission conducted a gospel-preaching service there as well, every night of the year, in which twenty-seven different churches and Christian groups participated. Twenty men, all of whom had professed faith in the Lord Jesus, stayed as permanent residents at the lodging house, and the staff helped them to grow in faith.

"One evening," said Donn Rainbolt, lodging house manager, "a man sat in my office and asked the Lord Jesus to save him. It was my privilege to help him trust the promises of God. He had been a heavy drinker, and his family did not want him around. He was eighty years old. Praise God, Christ found him."

During 1977, chapel attendance totaled 9,676, lodgings were provided for 1,047, free meals were served to 32,639, and 7,674 free pieces of clothing were given away. The statistics reflected the number of men who were sin-sick, physically ill in some instances, from broken homes, living from one drunken binge or drug spree to the next. These numbers represent local homeless men, transients, migrant workers, and parolees.

In the closing months of 1978, the roster was full at the men's residence lodging, with an increase in younger men in the program. One evening, three residents responded to the invitation at the close of the service, seeking a closer walk with the Lord. The oldest of the three was only twenty-two. Unknown to us, one of them, Rob, had been absent-without-leave from the military for several months. Donn Rainbolt, resident superintendent, wrote a letter for Rob, testifying to his rehabilitation. Rob took the letter with him when he turned himself in.

Terry was a bit older, but the staff believed that he

had a lot of potential and that God was at work in Terry's life. He had some difficult times after coming to the residence, including the loss of a young son in a tragic accident. The staff believed that God used the Mission to help Terry bear up under his trials in a way that was consistent with his testimony.

The women's ministry welcomed a new part-time director in 1977. One day, a young expectant mother came into the Mission and asked the new director, "Weren't you a leader in Pioneer Girls at one time?"

Miss Eleanor Tuinstra had, indeed, been that leader. Eleanor had come to the Mission in 1956 and began her ministry as the director of family work, serving seven years. She resigned in 1963 when she married Rev. George Bontekoe. Fourteen years later, she returned on a part-time basis to the same position.

Said Eleanor, "The work is still challenging but different—sometimes frustrating and often encouraging. I am most grateful that I have the privilege of being a representative of Jesus Christ to those who come in contact with the Mission."

Superintendent Henry Hoekstra shared Eleanor's sentiments. "As Christians, we know the problem is sin," he said. "The solution is Jesus Christ . . . and Mel Trotter Mission has been making the solution known for seventy-seven years."

Records tell the story of success. Hundreds of men and women have come to know Jesus Christ as their Savior because the Mel Trotter Mission reached out with the message. Many of those people are now in full-time service, repeating the same message.

One such person was a nine-year-old lad named Robert McCarthy. When he grew up, Robert trained at Moody Bible Institute, then he and his wife, Frances, served as faith missionaries in Kentucky. After that, Robert served as pastor in Baptist churches in Indianapolis, Indiana; Dayton, Ohio; Winston-Salem, North Carolina; and then at Eastmont Baptist Church in Grand Rapids, Michigan.

At the 1976 annual January Bible conference, Robert McCarthy, coming full circle, conducted the noon-day services. Who could have imagined at the first Bible conference in 1900, that seventy-eight years later the Old Lighthouse would still be hosting the event.

For the 1978 January Bible conference, J. Stratton Shufelt served as song leader and soloist. His name was well-known in evangelistic and music circles. He was associated with Dr. A. W. Tozer in Chicago and for nine years was minister of music at the Moody Memorial Church, working with Dr. Harry Ironside.

By 1979, the Bible conference schedule changed. It would no longer be held during January—which always included the nineteenth, Mel Trotter's spiritual birthday—but instead would be conducted in the fall to avoid the heavy January snows.

In those days, the cost of reaching out to the lost and needy—paying utility bills, doing the laundry, serving good meals, and maintaining the lodging house—was a burden. But God's people were ever loyal in their prayers and in giving gifts of food, used clothing, and money—all of it needed every day of every week. Since its founding in 1900, the Mission never had a membership but was entirely dependent on donations from the public for the operation of its various ministries. Over the years, the demand for additional services was constant and ever increasing, for there was never an end to the needs of the less fortunate and the transients who came to the doors of the Mission. Without the faithful interest and prayers of the Lord's people, it would have been impossible to continue in the Lord's work.

The work of Mel Trotter Mission and the objective of its ministry is found in the apostle Paul's testimony in 1 Corinthians 15:3-4, "For I delivered unto you first of all that which I also received, how that Christ died for our sins according to the scriptures; and that he was buried, and that he rose again the third day according to the scriptures."

When Mel Trotter came to Grand Rapids in 1900, he came to bring a message of salvation to the forgotten men and women in our society.

"They still come," said Superintendent Hoekstra, in the following words he penned.

> They come. . . and come, from various parts of the world, from all walks of life.
> Some are members of churches—and preachers.
> Some have degrees in higher education.
> Some have prison records.
> Some have been hurt seriously—marred for life.
> Some have been married—now divorced.
> Some have children, long forsaken.
> Some are men, others women.
> Some young, others old.
> Some are running from someone or something,
> But all are running from God.
> Some have heard something about God,
> But none seem to know Him.
> They come . . . and come, all come to the Mission for something.
> All have needs, but all do not know what they need.
> All men, women, and children who come are helped in various ways.
> All are shown the love of Jesus Christ our Lord, then
> All are told of the love of Jesus.
> All hear the gospel explained.
> All do not believe; some confess they do.
> All are challenged to a better way of life by faith in the Lord Jesus Christ.

Praise God the seed planted here in hearts prepared
   by the Holy Spirit does bear fruit.
Hearts are changed and lives are rearranged by the
   Grace of God.

For seventy-eight years, the purpose and the objective of the Mission had remained the same because the
ministry had been administered by godly individuals
who knew and loved the Lord, and by staff members
who had a God-given burden to be a present help in
time of need.

Just such a one needing help was Carl, a troubled
young man who came to the Mission one day in 1978.
His clothes were shabby, and he seemed hopeless and
defeated. After a few weeks, Carl said he wanted a better way of life, and he became intensely interested in
the gospel. At the close of our evening service, he went
forward to accept Jesus Christ as His Lord and Savior.
Carl became a good helper around the Mission, and
other residents and all of the staff loved him.

When he received word that his father was dying of
cancer in Denver, Colorado, Carl wanted very much to
be at his father's side and to tell him of the new life he
had in Jesus Christ. Fellow residents collected money
to buy a ticket, and the Mission also contributed. What
a reunion. A dying father and a saved son!

Whether it is 1900 or 1978, God works the same—His
love and His Spirit never change. But as the 1970s drew
to a close, watchers of the social scene felt that the
church was becoming more involved in reconstructing
society, and they questioned the relevance of rescue
missions. To the doubters, one minister in particular, a
man named John, would say, "What would you do with
me? I was a drunk. I had not finished my education. I
could not hold a job. I had been in many hospitals to
be dried out and went right back to the bottle again as

soon as I was discharged. I had been in jails for drunkenness clear across America."

One evening, John was walking along the banks of
the Grand River in Grand Rapids, Michigan. He was
thinking about throwing himself in the water when
someone put a gospel tract in his hand and invited him
to the Mel Trotter Mission.

"It looked warm and inviting," said John, "and I had
nowhere else to go. I went into the Mission that evening,
heard the gospel preached for the first time and gave
my heart to Christ. My whole life was transformed. I
finished my education and now I am a minister of the
gospel. Would you consider that irrelevant?"

The Mel Trotter Mission is extremely relevant today—
and it will continue to be relevant in the tomorrows.
Through it, Christians have a unique opportunity to
serve our risen, living Christ.

The Mel Trotter Mission continues to reach out and
will continue to be there. As long as the poor are among
us, as long as lost souls need a Savior, the Mel Trotter
Mission will be everlastingly at it.

Agnes Gezon Remembers

I am now eighty-seven years old. During the Depression,
our family did not have money for a vacation, but my
mother said that if she could attend the annual Bible
conference at the City Rescue Mission, it would be a
wonderful vacation.

I had attended meetings with her and understood her
request. I had heard Mel Trotter tell the story of his conversion. I heard Hammontree and Rodeheaver lead the
audience in song. I heard a speaker from England speak
on the wonders of creation.

Through the years at family gatherings, we would

laugh as Mother told us about her vacation. One of our younger brothers was with her, and they sat in the first row of the balcony. The speaker was well into his message when he said something that elicited a loud "amen" from Casey Vander Jagt. Mother grabbed little brother as he leaned over the railing to see the man with the booming voice.

Through the years, our family has followed the activities of the Mission. It is a beacon in our city, and we thank God for your vision.

On the Threshold

WHAT IS LONELINESS? Loneliness doesn't keep a calendar, and Mission workers in Grand Rapids had been meeting lonely people since the days of the old City Rescue Mission in 1900.

In 1982, Superintendent Henry Hoekstra wrote about loneliness and fellowship in a moving piece that appeared in the *Mission Messenger:*

> What about a young man who sobbed, "If I should die nobody would cry for me." He had just received word that his young sister, his only living relative, had been killed in a tragic accident in Chicago. Is this loneliness?
>
> An elderly woman came to the Mission and asked if she could have a suit of clothes for her husband who had died that morning. She had no money to buy him a proper suit. She wept while telling us of her coming loneliness. He was placed in a coffin wearing a suit from the Mission. Is this loneliness?
>
> The Mission has many children in our youth ministries who do not know their real parents. They are forsaken, unloved, and often alone. Is this loneliness?
>
> There are hundreds of men, women, and chil-

dren who are hungry, homeless, and friendless. Is this loneliness?

"My baby is hungry. I just need some food for her. Nobody seems to care!" Is this loneliness?

These are some of the often forgotten, forsaken, destitute, and heart-touching examples of the people we are helping daily.

But the lonely people are the hundreds who come to us and are not in fellowship with God, unconscious to the voice of God's love and mercy, living a life void of worshiping God, having no knowledge of forgiveness of sin! This is true loneliness.

Man was created to know God and to experience fellowship and joy in Jesus Christ, God's Son. John 17:3 reads, "And this is life eternal, that they might know thee, the only true God, and Jesus Christ, whom thou hast sent."

When the lonely men and women about whom Rev. Hoekstra wrote came to the Mel Trotter Mission, they stood on the threshold of fellowship with God. The compassion for those who came is evident in Henry Hoekstra's words. Through the years, the Lord had provided the Mission with, as Robert Kregel, president of the Mission Board of Directors said, "the kind of leadership a ministry such as this needs. Dealing with personal and family problems day after day takes a uniquely gifted person of God.

"God has given us great men particularly suited for this work, beginning with Mel Trotter, and later such men as Fred Zarfas, Claude Moore, George Bontekoe, and Henry Hoekstra."

Rev. George Bontekoe, who had been superintendent for thirty years, had retired six years before but had continued his association with the Mission as part-time chaplain. Because of physical problems, Rev. Bontekoe found it necessary to completely retire as of February 1, 1983. His wife, Eleanor Bontekoe, continued as director of the family ministry, a work that continued to expand. The Mission never stopped reaching into homes and counseling those who came for help.

Mr. Henry Hoekstra had succeeded Rev. Bontekoe as superintendent, and Henry proved to be a man with significant business ability as well as a personal concern for the souls of people. "Under his leadership," noted Robert Kregel, "the ministry of the Mission continued to grow and expand, and the confidence of the Christian community in the Mission has grown under his capable leadership."

In 1982, Hoekstra advised the Mission board that the work had become too strenuous for him, and he asked them to seek a replacement. Hoekstra recommended that the board consider Jim Lenters, who had been serving as Henry's assistant.

The board accepted Hoekstra's recommendation, and Jim Lenters was welcomed as the new executive director (what was once called superintendent). Jim had served on the Mission staff for seven years and was thus familiar with the ministry. No one doubted his commitment to God, which showed through both his compassion for the needy and his passion for souls

Jim's wife, Darlene, worked as the Mission's office secretary. These two workers for the Lord felt called to serve Him in rescue mission ministry.

The fall of 1984 brought mixed emotions. First, the annual Bible conference was discontinued. The conference had its beginning in the early days of Mel Trotter's ministry, and its termination marked the end of an era. But the future is in the young people, and there was joy to be found in the reports from Camp Mel-Tro-Mi. By the end of the summer, a former gang member confessed Christ as Lord of his life, a formerly timid young girl received the power to testify with boldness on behalf of her Lord, another individual's attitude of defiance toward the gospel was replaced by an increased sense of reverence for the name of God, and one who came seeking a peace within her life found that for which she was looking.

Change at the Mission, it seems, is not only inevitable but also frequent. After serving as executive director for five years, Jim Lenters stepped down from that position in 1988 to become acting chaplain. Later, Jim left to take a position at the Holland Rescue Mission.

Replacing Jim, Harold Koning joined the Mission as executive director. After Harold had served for a time, he said, "Friends ask me, 'What's it like to be the director of Mel Trotter Ministries? How's it going?' I tell them, 'Hard to describe,' and then a smile suffices for most inquiries as the conversation switches back to a world they're more familiar with."

But one might well wonder, What *is* it really like? "Men, young people, families, and even prostitutes come to Mel Trotter Ministries. These people could quite easily get the same food, clothing, and items at no cost elsewhere, without having to sit through a chapel exercise or hear one-on-one of God's love."

The Mission offers something else, something true and lasting. "People come to the Mission and realize, 'There's more than the street, broken homes, and my problems,'" said Harold. "What's it like? Humbling, to see how sin corrupts and destroys people; encouraging, to see how God can change a life. I read my Bible with new insights as I work here."

During Harold Koning's time as executive director, Rev. Leonard McElveen came on staff. Leonard said that Galatians 2:20 epitomized his existence in a very personal way: "I am crucified with Christ: nevertheless I

live; yet not I, but Christ liveth in me: and the life which
I now live in the flesh I live by the faith of the Son of
God, who loved me, and gave himself for me."

"This passage of Scripture, the message of the un-
leashing power of the gospel, first came across my path
back in 1973," said Leonard. "At that time, I was a drug
lord on the East Coast attempting to use power, position, and money as a means to inner fulfillment."

Leonard once stood on the threshold of destruction,
but through various means Jesus Christ invited Leonard
to leave the drug world and enter the kingdom of God.
"I realized my sin and asked for forgiveness," Leonard
said, "and now my life is changed."

Rev. McElveen received his training at the Syracuse
University Evangel College, and at schools in the Bronx,
New York. His previous ministries included a prison
ministry, an associate pastorate, and a foster home care
ministry.

Rev. McElveen's work at the Mission was largely with
the eighteen- to twenty-nine-year-old resident men. Most
of these young men have problems with both alcohol
and drugs. Over the period of their ninety-day stay at
the residence, they study their Bibles, hear lectures having to do with their problems of addiction, and learn
biblical principles of discipline. The majority of these
men make professions of faith in Christ, and, in general, make good progress. The Mission workers intro-
duce them to local churches and help them further their
education.

Among the people who have witnessed the redemption of lives is George Bontekoe. "It has been thirty-five
years," said George, "that the Lord has allowed me to
serve Him at the Mel Trotter Mission—and Eleanor almost as many years."

And what George summarizes as his Mission experience is true for all of us who have served: "We had our

joys and sorrows—our laughter and tears—our encouragements and discouragements. Such is life. How true are the words of Psalm 126:3: The Lord hath done great things for us [and in us and through us]; whereof we are glad.'"

The Lord did great things through Harold Koning, and he made a lasting impression on those to whom he ministered. But Harold served for little more than a year. Then, in 1989, Richard Roberds accepted the Board's invitation to become the executive director of Mel Trotter Ministries. He began his duties on August 14.

Harold Koning's friends had asked him, "Why do they come?" Richard Roberds's friends asked a different question. "How can you work with those people?" Richard's answer was, "The longer I work here, the stranger that question sounds. It is a privilege to minister to those people and to call many of them friends. God has helped our staff see past the ragged appearance of the men, women, and children we serve, and to see that they are really no different from us. They hurt the same as we do, they laugh much like we do, and they shed the same kind of tears."

Richard acknowledged that when down-and-out people come to us in the beginning, they are different from those who work at the Mission. "The only real difference," he said, "is the shepherd they follow, and that's why we're here. Each day we give these friends a glimpse at the Good Shepherd, and I can't begin to tell you how exciting it is when someone turns to follow Him."

As the 1980s came to a close, the words of Psalm 77:11 seemed appropriate: "I will remember the works of the Lord: surely I will remember thy wonders of old." The works of the Lord through the Mel Trotter Mission and its programs are indeed a wonder. And few programs have had more impact on the city of Grand Rapids than some of those that were begun in the early years of Mel

Trotter's ministry: the citywide Bible class, the radio ministry, and the Maranatha Men's Fellowship.

Consider the outreach of what was first called the City Bible Class and later became known as the Friday Night Bible Class. The first teacher to conduct these classes was Dr. James M. Gray, president of the Moody Bible Institute. He came every week by train from Chicago. Dr. P.W. Philpott, a renowned Bible teacher of that time, was another teacher in those early years.

Then Dr. William "Billy" McCarrell came on the scene. He was pastor of the Cicero Bible Church in Cicero, Illinois, and for nine years he traveled from Chicago every week to teach the class. In those days, there was a great emphasis on the assurance of salvation and on the premillennial return of Christ. Many people came directly to the Mission from work to be sure of getting a seat to listen to the teaching on those provocative subjects.

For several years, the class was taught by different teachers who were able to serve for only short periods of time. Then began the ministry of Dr. David D. Allen, pastor of Calvary Baptist Church in Hazel Park, Michigan. For twenty-one years the people of Grand Rapids were blessed with one of the best practitioners of expository Bible teaching.

Pastor Allen backed all of his statements with Scripture that he quoted from memory. He always gave the reference, then quoted the verse, followed again by the reference. And he never misquoted or missed the correct chapter and verse of Scripture.

Through the years, Pastor Allen taught—and taught thoroughly—2 Corinthians, Galatians, Ephesians, 1 Thessalonians, 1 Timothy, Hebrews, and, for two seasons, Romans. Those who attended faithfully received Bible study equal to anything offered at any Bible school, for Dr. Allen also taught for many years at the Detroit Bible College.

Dr. Allen possessed wonderful discipline concerning time. At eight o'clock, he began his teaching, and for one solid hour he taught. If people needed to call a cab for transportation, they could prearrange with the cab company for nine. The cab would be there just as the meeting was dismissed.

At nine o'clock, Dr. Allen would say, "I see by the clock that time has failed us." He put a little mark in his Bible at the verse where he was teaching and closed the service with prayer. The following week at eight o'clock he began by saying, "Last week, when time failed us . . ." and he started in right where he left off the week before.

Following Dr. Allen's twenty-one years, the class was taught by Rev. Charles R. Svoboda, who was on the staff at Grand Rapids School of the Bible and Music. He taught for two years, then because of changing social attitudes, the attendance dwindled, and the Friday Night Bible class was discontinued. The record of about seventy years of solid Bible teaching, however, had a telling effect on Grand Rapids and the surrounding area.

Along with other fine musicians, I served as organist for all of those years. I count this as one of the great blessings in my life.

Early in 1937, the City Rescue Mission went on the air in Grand Rapids with a program called *Morning Mission*. The station call letters were WASH, which later merged with WOOD radio and became one station. In the early days, though, the call letters in the morning were WASH and at noon the station was identified as WOOD. Later, the call letters WASH were dropped altogether.

Morning Mission was first conducted by Rev. Herbert Farrar, who was on the Mission staff. He conducted the program live every weekday morning from seven to seven-thirty. for three years. A live broadcast made it necessary for those who had a part in the program to get an early start on the day, even in the dead of winter. But through their efforts, the program was a special blessing to many of the listeners who had this refreshing start.

When Rev. Farrar left, the broadcast was conducted by Mel Johnson, who came on staff just before the homegoing of Mel Trotter.

In 1954, the Mission completed negotiations with William Kuiper, who had sold his clothing business to buy a radio station. Beginning Monday morning, March 1, 1954, from seven-fifteen to seven-thirty *Morning Mission* was heard on a new station, WFUR. Kuiper stated that "the primary goal of WFUR is to keep telling the story of love, that all who believe might receive salvation."

For years, the broadcast began with the theme song, "Jesus Is the Sweetest Name I Know," and it closed with Homer Hammontree and Rev. Paul Beckwith singing "Just Keep on Praying Till the Light Breaks Through."

By 1990, the radio program had become a five-minute spot called *Living Free*, still on WFUR.

The Maranatha Men's Fellowship began in the mid-1930s with a group of a dozen or so Christian businessmen. They met at noon for prayer, Bible study, and fellowship on the second floor of a Chinese restaurant at the corner of Lyon Street and Monroe Avenue, across from the old Pantlind Hotel. They called their group Maranatha, meaning *O Lord, come.*

The early group consisted of, among others, Pat and Bernie Zondervan, Chris Sonneveldt Sr. and his sons, Louis Kregel, Harry Wiersina, Peter Quist, Herbert Montgomery, Ted Engstrom, Lewis Steenwyk, and Tony Sietsma.

During World War II, because of gas and food rationing and difficulty finding parking places downtown, the group moved to the YMCA. Because of the war, however, attendance went to an all-time low.

In 1966, when Mel Trotter Mission moved to the Commerce Avenue site, the Mission gave Maranatha Men's Fellowship a room in the lower auditorium. The noon attendance by that time had grown to between eighty and ninety men each week, and a group of volunteer women from the Mission prepared a luncheon at a cost of three dollars per person, which included dessert and beverage.

The objectives of Maranatha Men's Fellowship group are to reach more men for Christ by proclaiming His saving grace at every opportunity; to live daily for the glory and honor of Christ; to share His love with those around them; to attend the luncheon faithfully; to invite associates, clients, and friends to attend; and to continue in prayer.

Mr. George Benes, ninety years of age in 1990, had been attending the meetings for almost fifty years. He said, "I come to hear good messages. It's a feeling of togetherness—a fellowship with people of like precious faith."

One active pastor who attended regularly said, "I enjoy hearing the good biblical messages. This is a time for me to be spiritually refreshed and renewed."

While the programs of the Mel Trotter Mission have left their mark on the community, so, too, have the Mission volunteers made vital contributions to the everyday, ongoing work of the ministries.

"It's hard to put into words the feelings I have toward our dedicated volunteer staff," said Randy Sharpe, director of development. "And when I say *dedicated*, I mean it in a very deep and involved sense. Some of the volunteers have worked with us for more than fifty years. But even new members are no less dedicated. One hundred plus volunteers make up the majority of Mission staff in a wide range of positions. Needless to say, we could not operate without them."

One special group of volunteers, for instance, are men

from a ministry called His Hands. This group of local craftsmen serve God by using their construction skills to do projects for other Mission ministries. They added twenty-two more beds to help with the ever-increasing number of homeless men who come in for shelter each night.

Ninety years of rescue work finds the Mission standing on the threshold of the twenty-first century.

Testimony of Roland Vaughn

I came to the Lord through my first contact with the Mel Trotter Mission when I was home recovering from a back injury. In the spring of 1953, I first tuned in on the *Morning Mission*—the daily radio broadcast of the Mission. I heard an invitation to attend evening services at the Branch Mission and, still unable to work, with time on my hands, I started to attend services two or three times a week.

Under sound gospel preaching, I soon became aware that salvation wasn't a matter of doing something for God; it was accepting as a gift something God had provided for me.

On February 18, 1954, at a Youth for Christ meeting at the Mission I accepted that gift, and the blood of Jesus Christ, God's Son, cleansed me from all sin. I was born again of God and am now living the new life. Eternal life! I think it could have been much earlier if I had been told about Jesus when I was a boy, instead of being given a whiskey toddy every morning.

CHAPTER TWENTY

Hope for the Hopeless

OUR COMMUNITY OFFERS myriad social programs. But
homeless people, people without hope, and people in
need are still seeking succor. There are no simple causes
or cures for social problems. Our culture, though, has
become conditioned to look for a quick fix. Then people
become bewildered when the quick fixes don't last, and
the moral breakdown of society continues.

We've seen moral confrontations over Supreme Court
nominations, a man accused of killing and then eating
his victims, and a steady increase of the HIV virus. Is it
any wonder that in a world of such disheartening realities people are seeking solutions? Is it any wonder that
people still come to Mel Trotter Ministries to find hope,
to find the solution of lasting value?

The Mission can lead the way to God's lasting solution, but Mel Trotter Ministries itself is not immune
to change. In 1991, Richard Roberds left his position
as executive director, and the Board of Directors appointed a familiar figure as interim director—Rev. Henry
Hoekstra.

Changes in directorship, though, have never interrupted God's work. Mark Schut, treasurer of the Board
of Directors remarked, "I have seen the Lord bless this
ministry beyond our expectations. We have seen living
stories of the Lord working in and changing lives, but

we know that it is not our hard work that brings the fruit but God's grace working through us."

The ministries at Mel Trotter Ministries just keep growing. The Mission outreach programs increase to serve the homeless, provide food to families, and minister to children through the camp and youth activities throughout the year. It's easy to get a warm feeling from touching so many lives. The Mission never loses sight, however, that its calling is to provide for the spiritual needs as well as the physical needs.

"There is a song," said Mark, "that reminds me of the ministry of Mel Trotter Ministries. In reference to persons who are outcast—the prostitute, the one going through divorce—the song asks the question, 'Who will be Jesus to them?' The world can only see Christ through us. It's our hope that through the efforts of Mel Trotter Ministries, many will see Him clearly and will take that first step to come to Him."

For the outcast, the prostitute, and the divorced to come to Him, it is necessary to have trained Mission workers guide the lost in taking that first step. Some of those workers find the task so rewarding that they want to make rescue mission work their career. To that end, Rev. John Willock developed the Mel Trotter School of Missions, which trains students for vocations in rescue ministries.

John had come on board as permanent executive director of Mel Trotter Ministries in October 1992. Entry into the Mel Trotter School of Missions is contingent upon graduating from the Mission's Christian Discipleship Program, which is part of the men's ministry. Some of the residents at the men's ministry have suffered terrible personal losses because of addiction to drugs and alcohol. As children, some of them experienced years of neglect, abuse, and rejection. The workers who minister to these men thank God for the opportunity, and they celebrate every victory.

Before entering the Christian Discipleship Program, a resident must live at the men's residence for at least a year. While living there, they submit to strict rules and regulations, receive one-on-one counseling, and complete a daily work assignment. They write daily devotionals based on a chapter of the Bible, and they attend daily classes in Bible and Christian living. Some of the men are disciplined because of rule infractions, but if they stay with the program, they graduate.

On February 10, 1993, five resident men graduated from the Christian Discipleship Program. They will be going to the School of Missions to be equiped for rescue mission ministry. Each student attends the school for one year, during which time they receive practical training in missions and academic instruction at one of the local colleges.

The five young men who graduated from the Christian Discipleship Program and went into the School of Missions are to be commended. They should consider their graduation a real accomplishment. The program isn't easy to finish, but, by the grace of God, they did it.

Rev. Willock had reason for joy in those five young men. It is hoped that he will experience similar success in his new position in Terre Haute, Indiana. Yes, in September of 1993, Mel Trotter Ministries was again looking for a new executive director. Donn Rainbolt acted in the interim and, in his quiet way, kept the operation running smoothly.

Little did Donn Rainbolt think when he joined the staff of the Mel Trotter Mission in September 1956 that he would still be working there in 1999. Donn's spiritual history began many years before 1956, and it would be remiss not to pay special tribute to Donn and his many years of faithful service.

Donn was born and reared in a non-Christian home and, at the age of thirteen, was still without any knowledge of either God's Word or His Son, Jesus Christ. "Then," said Donn, "I found an old Gideon Bible, and the providence of God led me to begin reading it. I read the first five books of the Old Testament and the first five books of the New Testament. God was using His Word in my life, but I still did not know the way to God."

Donn eventually wandered away from reading the Bible. He did not know any Christians, but the Lord sent some along. "A few zealous Christians came into our neighborhood to set up a child evangelism class. On November 27, 1949, I was clearly shown for the first time the way of salvation through Christ. That day I asked the Lord Jesus to come into my life. The night of sin was over—the dawn of hope entered my life."

Then one day Rev. Bontekoe noticed Donn and his wife, Alice, passing out tracts in front of our men's shelter, then located on Monroe Avenue. Donn joined the staff—as did Alice, after their children were grown and on their own—serving the Mission in various positions from one-on-one counseling to Sunday school bus driver.

Donn would be the first to admit that his work at Mel Trotter Ministries is not one continuous string of victories, and he has seen the workload increase with each new year. "God gives enabling grace with each responsibility," said Donn, "so that I can say, 'His commandment is not grievous.' He faithfully meets every need in my life. The Lord has enabled me to receive some good Christian training for which I am thankful. Then He has added other wonderful blessings in allowing me to work for the Mission."

Donn's association with Mel Trotter Ministries is one of the longest on record. Rev. George Bontekoe spent thirty-five years working in various capacities at the Mission. Mel Trotter completed forty years. But Donn passed the forty-year mark, and, as of this writing, he is still everlastingly at it!

For rescue mission workers in the nineties, remaining at it is sometimes a challenge, albeit a rewarding one. It seemed fitting, then, that in 1994 the name of the Mission newsletter became the *Challenge*. And the summer 1994 edition announced another change: Mel Trotter Ministries welcomed Rev. Thomas J. Laymon as their new executive director.

Rev. Laymon and his wife, Janice, moved here from the Detroit area after he had served for five years as one of the administrators of the Detroit Rescue Mission Ministries. While there, he developed, among other things, a new shelter for homeless women and their dependent children and two new programs for women with substance abuse.

When asked of his vision for Mel Trotter Ministries, Tom replied, "It is my desire to see an additional thirty-five spaces in our men's residential program this summer, which will allow for an additional one hundred men each year. We want to encourage the men who are presently just staying overnight to join the residency programs and begin dealing with the issues in their lives."

Tom could see another need as well. "I see a real need in this community for a shelter to house homeless and hurting women and their children. Like the men, these women also need hope in dealing with substance abuse problems. I want to see Mel Trotter Ministries once again become the heart of evangelism in this city."

The Mission was well placed to become that heart. The neighborhood surrounding the Old Lighthouse main building had for some time been called the Heartside District. During 1994, Mel Trotter Ministries became the first organization serving in the Heartside District to be given a license by the State of Michigan's Center for Substance Abuse Services (CSAS), which entitled the Mission to provide residential substance abuse treatment.

The Mission substance abuse treatment consists of a four-level program implemented by a qualified staff of counselors. Each of the four levels includes a spiritual dimension to help every participant become a healthy member of society. The State CSAS-approved-and-licensed program is offered to anyone regardless of race, religion, or economic status.

Other events besides the CSAS program put Mel Trotter Ministries in the spotlight. In July the Mission held the "Biggest Bar-B-Q in Town" and fed more than four hundred people from the Heartside District. Several people responded to the gospel message.

In August 1994, the Mission initiated an annual back-to-school day. The first year, three hundred people attended, and the children were outfitted with new school clothes. In 1995, the event hosted four hundred people, and by 1998, more than one thousand adults and children attended. The Mission equipped more than five hundred severely underprivileged children with new clothes and school supplies such as pencils, paper, and notebooks. The children played games and sang songs, but the back-to-school-day is about more than fun. In 1998, thirty children and five adults made their decisions for Christ.

With thoughts of a new school year, the holidays cannot be far behind. The Mission had for years served a traditional holiday meal. But by the nineties the diners had become so numerous that it had become necessary to serve the Thanksgiving meal in the giant Grand Center in Grand Rapids.

Never before had the Mission been required to take on such a task for the Lord. Yet the West Michigan community, through volunteers and donors, enabled the Mel Trotter Ministries to feed several hundred homeless, hungry, and needy people. And best of all, in 1997, thirty-two people accepted Rev. Tom Laymon's invitation to become personally acquainted with Jesus Christ.

At Christmas, an estimated fourteen hundred families receive food and other items from the Mission. But the Christmas Adopt-a-Family program enables Mel Trotter Ministries to create special holidays for particularly needy families. Each family member makes a wish list, and people from the community adopt a family and provide them with gifts, food baskets, turkeys, and Christmas trees with all of the trimmings. The Adopt-a-Family program began with a list of twenty families and has grown to more than two hundred families.

Throughout the holidays and the associated activities, Tom Laymon never lost sight of his primary vision for Mel Trotter Ministries—the establishment of a residential facility for woman and children. In April 1995, he shared that vision with the nearly four hundred people who attended the Mission's spring banquet held at Calvary Church. "The population of homeless women and children has been increasing rapidly," said Tom. "We have been constantly praying for additional facilities that would allow us to minister to women, children, and families."

On December 18, 1995, God answered those prayers. Mel Trotter Ministries purchased the four-story John K. Burch building, a neighbor of the Mission. Two parties made the purchase possible. First, as a donation to Mel Trotter Ministries, the John K. Burch Company reduced the price of their building by two hundred thousand dollars. Second, H. J. (Hale) Mackay made a generous donation of $290,000 to the Mission.

The Mission could at last expand and open its doors for many homeless, hurting women and their children. The Burch building more than doubles the physical plant of Mel Trotter Ministries and will eventually include living space, classrooms, fitness rooms, a library, and much-needed office space. This facility would offer an unlimited stay to its residents in order to help them reenter life completely free of drugs and alcohol. And a food-service teaching kitchen would provide skill development to residents, enabling them to enter the workplace without depending on government aid.

There was good news as well from the men's CSAS residential treatment program. On February 21, 1996, twenty-one men graduated and are now finding jobs, housing, transportation, and fellowship with other Christians in local churches. Among those still in the program, many have made decisions for Christ.

Still, Mel Trotter Ministries must keep pace with the changing face of the community. The Mission started a new Spanish men's Bible study, and many of its members have accepted Christ as Savior.

The nineties also brought progress in the area of young people. At Camp Mel-Tro-Mi, well over two hundred children spend a week away from the pressures of the inner city each year. And each year an average of one hundred children made decisions to receive Christ. The summer of this writing, nearly two hundred decisions for Christ were made.

On Labor Day of 1995, the Mission held the first annual alumni reunion of the CSAS treatment program. Nearly thirty alumni were present, and after the meal the men shared stories about the life-changing and life-saving differences they've experienced as a result of their stay at the Mission.

At the second reunion, many of the alumni brought their families. As the CSAS program progresses, it becomes evident that men who were once without hope are no longer hopeless; those who were once alienated from their loved ones are forging new bonds of love and trust.

It takes a lot of work to restore something that has been all but destroyed. But restoring lives is what God is all about. So at Mel Trotter Ministries, the work goes on.

Testimony of Tom McQuade

I received the Lord as my personal Savior at the Mel Trotter Branch Mission on the night of September 3, 1954. For years I had been drinking heavily, which, of course, was the wrong thing to do, but trying to reform myself had not helped. I was a very troubled and confused man and was almost ready to give up.

As I walked into the Mission that night, Rev. Don Price was giving the invitation. It went something like this: "There are many men here tonight who have tried almost everything to quit their drinking habit and have not succeeded. They have never given the Lord a chance to come into their lives and help them. Why not give Him that chance tonight?"

I went forward and received Christ as my Savior. It was amazing how He changed my life. He gave me a new life, and since that day I have had no desire for alcohol or the things of the old life. And with the Lord helping me, I never will.

I thank Him every day for saving my soul and changing my life. He is a wonderful Savior!

The Best Is Yet to Be

ON FATHER'S DAY IN 1997, Charley Vandenberg played golf—for twenty-four hours! Charley was not indulging a mania for the game, he was participating in an event called the Golf Marathon of Hope, raising money for Mel Trotter Ministries' family rescue project. The event resulted in gifts and pledges totaling eighty-five thousand dollars.

When asked why he played the Golf Marathon of Hope, Charley replied, "Because I want to help homeless and struggling women and children, and I want to help Mel Trotter Ministries with the good they do in West Michigan."

Charley again gave of his time and energy in 1998 and raised more than eighty thousand dollars. By enduring this grueling event, Charley would help provide a residential facility for women and their children, where women would break free from substance abuse through the Ministries' CSAS treatment program, acquire skills, get help in finding jobs, and learn to strengthen their spirits—all part of the Mission's Christian Discipleship Program.

In 1996, Mel Trotter Ministries acquired a building for the women's shelter, but a lot of work remained to be done to turn the building into a residence. Many volunteers rolled up their sleeves to help prepare the new facility. The building's interior—fifty-five thousand square feet—had to be demolished before renovation could begin. A lot of dust flew at the corner of Commerce Avenue and Cherry Street as workmen and equipment bustled in and out of the building.

The Mission wanted to create a home-like environment, not a dormitory. To that end—as well as to finance the remodeling—the Mission initiated the Adopt-a-Room program. Those who donated funds to complete one residence room in the facility were given creative license in designing the room's layout and in buying furnishings. The one stipulation was that the decor of the entire shelter had to feel like a home to clients.

The new shelter would also house offices and rooms for religious and vocational training. Residents could take classes on meal preparation in a food-service training kitchen; they could learn computer proficiency in a state-of-the-art learning center, where reading, writing, and business math would also be taught; they could earn GED and high-school diplomas; and they could work out in a half-court gymnasium.

While mothers worked and studied, their children would be cared for in a playroom—designed as the result of a stolen wallet!

When Shirley Fleischmann, a professor of engineering at Grand Valley State University, discovered that her wallet was missing, she immediately canceled her credit cards and never expected to see her wallet again. Several weeks later, she received a telephone call from a construction worker with the Dan Vos Company. He had found her wallet on the construction site where he was working—the Mel Trotter Women and Children's Shelter.

Shirley came to the site and recovered her wallet, which was intact minus, of course, the cash. She inquired about the project and learned that rooms of the facility were available for "adoption."

With a design background that included building play-rooms for children, Shirley decided to invest. She said, "I just thought there must be something I could do, or else I wouldn't have been called there in that way."

As a result, the new shelter's playroom was designed by students from Grand Valley State University and Calvin College's American Society of Mechanical Engineers program, where Fleischmann serves as faculty adviser.

Shirley didn't question the circumstances that brought her to Mel Trotter's door. She said, "I just think that you're occasionally given signs you cannot ignore."

The first week of June marked the culmination of much work and prayer. The new Mel Trotter Ministries Women and Children's Shelter was ready for dedication. It was a particularly hectic time, because that week Mel Trotter Ministries also hosted the eighty-fifth annual conference of the International Union of Gospel Missions (IUGM). It was the largest conference in more than thirty years, with 860 registrants—plus their families—from rescue missions large and small.

The official dedication of the shelter was to take place on Friday. It had been a wet and rainy week, but on Friday, June 5, the rain stopped and the sun came out. IUGM conference attendees—hundreds of rescue mission workers from all over the world—stayed to witness the dedication. So many people attended, in fact, that the street had to be blocked off.

Men, women, and children of all ages and ethnic groups gathered in front of the shelter. The crowd included donors, volunteers, dignitaries, pastors, Heartside neighbors, representatives from other nonprofit organizations that serve the disadvantaged, the media, and interested people from all over West Michigan.

A giant gold ribbon stretched across the entrance of the shelter. When it was cut, just a little more than a year from the time the project started, the Board of Directors and staff of Mel Trotter Ministries saw a decade-old dream fulfilled. The Women and Children's Shelter is the largest and most comprehensive shelter in West Michigan, offering the growing population of homeless women and children an opportunity to find refuge and hope for a new life.

People and groups who had adopted rooms acted as hosts, guiding visitors through rooms that could be described only as breathtaking in their quality, decor, and personalization. Everyone who went through the building during the open house—unable to adequately express all that had been accomplished—could only murmur, "God does indeed answer prayers. A dream is now a reality."

Wilma Brewer was appointed director of the new shelter. Wilma attended the Grand Rapids School of the Bible and Music, and following graduation she trained with the New Tribes Institute of Fredonia, Wisconsin. After completing course work at the Language and Linguistics Institute in Camdenton, Missouri, she served with New Tribes Missions in Papua New Guinea for fifteen years as a translator, teacher, and community service worker.

Wilma was well served by her many years of experience in dealing with community relations. "An angry spirit existed among several of the women at the shelter," said Wilma. "Much gossip and many hurt feelings emerged from years of unresolved issues, bitterness, and abuse."

Wilma prayed with the women involved and instructed each one to read Hebrews 10:15–25: "I will put my laws in their hearts"; and Psalm 51: "Create in me a clean heart, O God."

One woman wanted to apologize for her angry spirit but admitted that she did not know how to get beyond her feelings of anger. She was directed to 1 Timothy 6:11 and encouraged to flee from the anger by running to God.

Another woman, Shelly, came to the shelter, hoping to regain custody of her children. Authorities had told her that she needed a rehabilitation program. Shelly tried everything to comply, but the possibility of having her kids again seemed impossible, and she felt hopeless. Shelter staff worked with the authorities and told them that the shelter could provide the program and a place for the woman and her children.

A counselor then showed Shelly one of the residence rooms and told her, "You and your children can stay here together." Shelly wept and jumped with joy as she realized that there was indeed hope. Her dreams were becoming a reality.

With many children residing in the new shelter, many of the mothers needed to learn interaction skills—such as patience. One mother asked, "How can I learn to be patient with my kids?" The counselor said, "Have patience with yourself first, with your child second, and steadfastly believe that the Lord will provide the power to be patient."

To the question "What are your highest hopes for the new women's program at Mel Trotter Mission?" Wilma Brewer replied, "That every woman and child who comes here will come to know Jesus Christ and trust Him to come into every part of their lives. If that happens, that leaves no doubt in my mind that their lives will be satisfying and they will not want to go back to the dangers of their past."

With the beginning of operations at the Women and Children's Shelter in 1998, the board and staff of Mel Trotter Ministries had much for which to be thankful. But there was one note of sadness in this year of much to celebrate. On November 9, 1998, Rev. George Bontekoe, at the age of eighty-nine, was called home to be with the Lord he loved and served for thirty-five years at Mel Trotter Ministries.

In 1953, George agreed to a three-month trial as superintendent and stayed on until 1975, when his health failed. George had a gentle spirit and once observed, "It is the material needs of the precious people, outcasts as far as some people are concerned, that sometimes frustrates me. The inability to ever do enough for the hungry, homeless, and suffering can be frustrating. Sure, some have used me, but you do what you can for Jesus' sake. I would not want to be in this work with a hard-nosed attitude. They are human beings for whom Christ died."

The solution for today's needs, according to George and Eleanor Bontekoe, is what it has always been—individual decisions to follow Jesus Christ.

As of this writing, it is 2000—the first year of the first decade of a new century and a new millennium. We don't know what the future holds, but the Lord still has all things under His control. As He was with the work in the past, He is with us now. And in the days ahead we can trust Him to accomplish His work through the ministry of His Word for those who are in need, not only materially but also spiritually.

Mel Trotter Ministries is often perceived as a soup kitchen. Yes, the Mission provides hot meals and shelter for approximately 230 men, women, and children each day. But the work of the Mission encompasses far more than food and shelter. The CSAS program, for instance, does not depend on state funding. Thus, the Mission is able to blend professional treatment with biblical teaching.

Because the residents voluntarily commit themselves to the program for nine to twelve months, they have time to see that living their lives according to the Word of God shifts their focus from addictive behavior—which kills emotional pain—to godly behavior—where pain can be healed.

Bill Small and Sally Walters came to the Mission at about the same time. They each wanted only a hot meal, but they both eventually decided to enter the CSAS treatment program. Bill went to the men's residence, and Sally and her children went to the Women and Children's Shelter.

A typical day for Bill and Sally begins at six in the morning with breakfast at seven. After breakfast, women who have children get their kids ready for school. Then all of the residents in both facilities begin working on chores—cleaning their rooms and common lavatories, making their beds, vacuuming, and straightening.

Then school is in session for the residents. Classes include money management, conflict resolution, anger management, parenting, the spiritual life, Overcomers (a Christ-centered twelve-step program), budgeting, meal planning, and morality, plus communication and thinking skills in the Mission's new computer-based learning center.

What usually begins with a bowl of soup often leads to graduation, aftercare, and the opportunity to make new life choices—choices that are pleasing to God.

Providing the lost and hopeless with new opportunities is what Mel Trotter Ministries is all about. But it is expensive. To meet the costs of saving lost lives, the Mission instituted a vehicle donation and resale program.

Through this program Mel Trotter Ministries accepts donated vehicles for reconditioning at the Vocational Vehicle Rehabilitation Center. Volunteer professionals at the center teach residents who are in recovery and rehabilitation programs to recondition the donated used vehicles. The Mission then offers them for sale, and the proceeds are used to help meet operating costs for the many programs sponsored by the Mission.

One might well ask, "A lot of money and effort are pumped into the programs and ministries at Mel Trotter. Do they work?" Rev. Tom Laymon, executive director of Mel Trotter Ministries, answers that question by relating the following incident:

> The other day I saw a sight that caused me to smile, and it warmed my heart. As I walked through the halls of the Mission, I saw one of our young mothers reading. Now most of you probably wonder why this prompted any response at all. Isn't this a rather normal human activity?
>
> This young mother came to us a few months ago with no hope in her eyes. She had many problems, not the least of which was that she didn't know Jesus as her Savior. However, it wasn't long until she opened her heart to the Lord. But there was another major block to her growth in the Christian life—she could not read.
>
> Soon after she came to our Women and Children's Shelter, we opened our new multimedia learning center. What I saw in that hallway was a young mother who, after only a few months, was reading. She chose a Christian book to open her heart and mind to the Holy Spirit. Not only had she gone from illiteracy to reading at a junior high level, but also the staff reports that her growth in Christ is moving even faster.

With all of the money and effort that are expended, does it work? Yes. Yes—it works! It works because through its many changes of address, Mel Trotter Ministries continues to be the Old Lighthouse, shining the light of Christian love into the darkness.

As the Mission faces the next millennium, the words of Robert Browning seem appropriate:

Grow old along with me!
The best is yet to be. . . .

In the year 2000, the Mission will be one hundred years old, but "the best is yet to be." And it will take eternity to comprehend what great things the Lord has done.

The first chapter of this book told about the redemption of a man named Mel Trotter. There can be no last chapter. The work goes on and will, with God's help, continue to the end of time. Only then will the Lord Himself reveal what He has accomplished down through the years, through all the thousands of faithful and committed workers. Our reward will be His "Well done, good and faithful servant."

So, until the Lord's return, we labor—everlastingly at it.

Inasmuch as ye have done it unto one of the least of these
my brethren, ye have done it unto me.
                                        (Matthew 25:40)

Chronology of Mel Trotter Ministries

1897   January 19—Mel Trotter accepts Christ as Savior
1900   (circa) The first Bible conference
1900   February—City Rescue Mission opens
1900   City Rescue Mission moves to Market Street
1902   A two-story addition added to Market Street location
1905   Mel Trotter ordained as a minister
1906   City Rescue Mission moves to the old Smith Opera House
1917   Mel Trotter begins a ministry to soldiers in World War I
1919   Mel Trotter experiences a time of trial
1924   May—Mel Trotter fills in for Billy Sunday in Memphis, Tennessee
1935   (circa) Formation of Maranatha Men's Fellowship
1937   City Rescue Mission initiates its *Morning Mission* radio program
1940   September 11—Mel Trotter goes home; City Rescue Mission becomes the Mel Trotter Mission; Shy becomes interim superintendent
1942   Mel Trotter Mission initiates wartime outreach
1944   Rev. Fred C. Zarfas appointed as superintendent of the Mel Trotter Mission

1945   Branch mission established to care for transient
        men
1946   Mission headquarters remodeled and repaired
1950   Golden Jubilee of the Mel Trotter Mission; Rev.
        Bob Ingersoll appointed as interim
        superintendent of Mel Trotter Mission
1951   January—Rev. John W. Kershaw appointed as
        interim superintendent of Mel Trotter Mission;
        September—Rev. Claude J. Moore appointed as
        superintendent of Mel Trotter Mission; October—
        Saturday morning children's Bible class initiated
1952   March—Winifred J. Larson appears at Mel Trotter
        Mission; August—Mission headquarters improved;
        September—citywide Friday Night Bible Class
        revived
1953   George Bontekoe appointed superintendent of Mel
        Trotter Mission
1955   Last annual Bible conference to be held at the
        Smith Opera House location; Bob Jones speaks at
        Bible conference
1956   Old Mission headquarters sold; Mission leases
        Heyman Building on Monroe Avenue as
        temporary quarters; Mission purchases Kent
        Theater and Oaks hotel properties for new
        permanent headquarters; October 18–21—
        dedication ceremonies for new permanent
        headquarters
1957   Annual Bible conference held in the new location;
        Branch Mission remodeled
1959   Mel Trotter Mission newsletter pays tribute to the
        women who have worked at the Mission
1961   July 29—Mrs. Bontekoe goes home
1963   April 6—Rev. George Bontekoe weds Miss Eleanor
        Tuinstra; Mr. and Mrs. Hale McKay donate
        building to Mel Trotter Mission
1966   Mel Trotter Mission displaced by urban renewal

1967 Homer "Ham" Hammontree goes home
1968 Open house of new Mission headquarters at
     Commerce Avenue
1970 Print shop
1973 Mel Trotter Mission acquires land for a children's
     Bible day camp
1974 Camp Mel-Tro-Mi holds its first activities as a
     children's Bible day camp
1975 Mel Trotter Mission's Diamond Jubilee; Henry J.
     Sonneveldt appointed as interim superintendent
1976 May—Rev. Henry Hoekstra appointed as
     superintendent of Mel Trotter Mission
1978 J. Stratton Shufelt appears as soloist at Bible
     conference
1979 Change of date for annual Bible conference from
     January to autumn to avoid heavy snows
1984 Jim Lenters appointed as new executive director
     (formerly superintendent) of Mel Trotter Mission;
     annual Bible conferences discontinued
1988 Harold Koning appointed as executive director of
     Mel Trotter Mission
1989 Richard Roberds appointed as new executive
     director of Mel Trotter Ministries
1992 May—Rev. Henry Hoekstra appointed as interim
     director of Mel Trotter Ministries; October—John
     Willock appointed as new executive director of
     Mel Trotter Ministries; Mel Trotter School of
     Missions started
1993 Rev. Donn Rainbolt appointed as interim director
     of Mel Trotter Ministries
1994 Newsletter gets a new name—the *Challenge;* new
     outreach programs initiated—State of Michigan's
     Center for Substance Abuse Services treatment
     (CSAS), "Biggest Bar-B-Q in Town" for the
     Heartside District, children's Back-to-School
     program; May—Rev. Thomas J. Laymon

appointed as new executive director of Mel
Trotter Ministries

1995 Mel Trotter Ministries purchases John K. Burch
      Building for new Women and Children's Shelter

1996 First alumni reunion of CSAS treatment program

1997 First annual golf marathon to benefit Women and
      Children's Shelter

1998 June—Mel Trotter Ministries hosts the International
      Union of Gospel Missions conference, and the
      new Women and Children's Shelter opening
      dedication ceremonies; November—Rev. George
      Bontekoe goes home

2000 Everlastingly at it!